THE KINGDOM OF GOD IS LIKE...

Other Books
by Thomas Keating

Awakenings

Reawakenings

Open Mind, Open Heart

The Mystery of Christ

Invitation to Love

THE KINGDOM OF GOD IS LIKE...

Thomas Keating

CROSSROAD • NEW YORK

1993

The Crossroad Publishing Company
370 Lexington Avenue, New York, NY 10017

Printed in the United States of America

Library of Congress Cataloging-in-Publication Data

Keating, Thomas
    The kingdom of God is like— /Thomas Keating
      p. cm.
    ISBN 0-8245-1363-0 (alk. paper)
    1. Jesus Christ—Parables—Sermons.   2. Jesus Christ—Words—
Sermons.   3. Catholic Church—Sermons.   4. Sermons, American.
I. Title.
BT375.2.K383   1993
226.8'06—dc20
                                    93-22706
                                    CIP

CONTENTS

FOREWORD

About a year after the publication of my *Hear Then the Parable,* I received a letter from a young minister in Northern Ireland involved in the peace movement, surely one of the most frustrating ministries around. He wrote that my analysis of the parable of the withered fig tree had spoken to his soul for it so accurately described his situation — he just keeps on manuring, hoping that somehow God will give life.

I wrote back thanking him for the letter, but saying that the credit should go to the parable teller, not the parable critic. The parable, not my exegesis, spoke to his soul. This is not some false humility, for I remember clearly the night I first worked up that section of the book. The parable did not impress me, since I thought it a minor one compared to some of the other ones. Furthermore, I was under some pressure to finish the chapter. I thought I knew Jesus' style and techniques as parable teller. As I mulled over the parable, I was struck by the futility of the man's effort, by the use of the term "manure" (actually more accurately "dung"), and by the ellipsis, which most translators fill in: "If it bears fruit, well...," and a shrug of the shoulders. Not much I thought, but typical of Jesus. More typical than I thought, because the stone the builder rejected has become the cornerstone. I'm delighted that Father Keating sees in this parable a symbol of the contemplative life.

Father Keating's *The Kingdom of God is Like* ... is itself elliptical like the parables. His sermons leave unsaid what should not be spoken and to the hearer the story's remainder. His style of preaching is immensely faithful to the parables, for he does not tell, but listens and joins his audience as co-hearers of the parables. Over and over again, he responds to the parable story with a story, each time leaving us to hear again. Or as Jesus challenged, "the one who has ears, had better hear."

Father Keating has four sermons on the parable of the leaven, one of the shortest and one might think least significant parables in the tradition, one on which even the evangelists do not comment. He seizes on the parable's radical nature, its unmasking of monumental evil. The parable is a lens on the everyday, exposing the presence of God where we dare not expect it, where we have been trained to ignore it. He sees miracle where it truly is. Not just in a mother's forgiveness of and caring for her son's murderer, but more importantly in the barely perceptible tear in the eye of the sociopath. For him the kingdom is not the bloom of a barren fig tree, but God's touch is enough.

By turning the parables over and over, Keating allows them to refocus the nonparabolic elements of the Jesus tradition. One might think that Jesus as King would be contrary to the monumental evil, the everydayness of the parables. But Keating shows they are of one piece, that Jesus's abandonment in death is the monumental evil and his resurrection is the mask that hides that abandonment, but exposes the miracle of God's great love.

We are perhaps too accustomed to think of the parables as simple stories for simple people. Such an attitude only cloaks our own arrogance. Keating restores Jesus as the artist of the soul, and he responds as an artist. One can only be astounded at how these parables continue to generate insights into the most profound issues of life.

BERNARD BRANDON SCOTT
Darbeth Distinguished Professor of New Testament
Phillips Graduate Seminary, Tulsa, Oklahoma

PREFACE

This third volume of homilies, following *Awakenings* and *Reawakenings*, owes much of its inspiration to the scholarly and insightful book by Bernard Brandon Scott, *Hear Then the Parable* (Fortress Press, 1989). The scripture texts given at the beginning of each chapter omit the settings and conclusions of the parables, which many exegetes believe to be the work of the evangelists themselves (see Funk, Scott, and Butts, *The Parables of Jesus: Red Letter Edition,* Sonoma, Calif.: Polebridge Press, 1988).

The laborious work of Scott and other scholars in seeking the original meaning of the parables brings into sharp focus aspects of Jesus' teaching and personality that have not been previously emphasized. When rightly understood, the parables help us to see how extraordinary a wisdom teacher Jesus really was, and how revolutionary, in the best sense of that word, was the content of what he taught and to which he bore witness by his life and death.

These insights cohere particularly well with the actual experience of people on the spiritual journey. When contemplative prayer is seriously embraced, we come upon the lived reality that Scott details so well: the reversal of expectations, the gradual and often painful liberation from emotional programs for happiness, and the increasing discovery of the kingdom of God in the ordinary and in the everyday. So often the experience of "corruption" — that which is first looked upon as crisis or catastrophe — is actually the occasion of the inbreaking of the kingdom, as God invites us to change not so much the situation as our attitudes.

I am grateful to Bernard Brandon Scott for allowing me to publish his ideas in popular form and to share the significant implications that I find in them for the following of Christ. And I am grateful to the first hearers of these homilies — the monks and the extended community at St. Benedict's Monastery, Snowmass, Colorado, and the many participants at Contemplative Outreach Intensive Retreats, where these ideas have first been aired and evaluated.

THOMAS KEATING

THE PARABLES OF THE KINGDOM

1

THE PARABLE OF
THE GOOD SAMARITAN

"A man was going down from Jerusalem to Jericho, and fell into the hands of robbers, who stripped him, beat him, and went away, leaving him half dead. Now by chance a priest was going down that road; and when he saw him, he passed by on the other side. So likewise a Levite, when he came to the place and saw him, passed by on the other side. But a Samaritan while traveling came near him; and when he saw him, he was moved with pity. He went to him and bandaged his wounds, having poured oil and wine on them. Then he put him on his own animal, brought him to an inn, and took care of him. The next day he took out two denarii, gave them to the innkeeper, and said, 'Take care of him; and when I come back, I will repay you whatever more you spend.'" (Luke 10:30–35)

To understand the full meaning of the parable of the good Samaritan, we need to be aware of the Jewish hierarchical society of the time. The priest, the Levite, and the ordinary Israelite or layperson were the familiar triad of that society. Sacred persons, places, and things were rigorously separated from the profane. Those who belonged to Israel —

15

insiders — were sharply distinguished from those who were not — outsiders.

Samaritans were not only looked upon as outsiders, but as the mortal enemies of the nation of Israel and apostates from the Jewish religion. They derived from the northern tribes of Israel and had split off from the rest of the nation during King David's reign. A rabbinical text of the time states that "one who eats the food of Samaritans is eating the food of swine," thus equating Samaritans as apostates from Judaism. For this parable's original audience, a Samaritan was the epitome of ultimate corruption.

As the parable begins, we hear that a traveler from Jerusalem to Jericho, presumably an Israelite, has been beaten up by robbers and left half dead by the roadside. Along come the various representatives of the hierarchical structure of that society. A priest sees the man and passes by. A Levite, a step down on the hierarchical ladder, also passes by.

The reason why the first two pass by the victim is not addressed. The law commanded that priests and Levites were not to bury the dead apart from their next of kin. But in this case the man was "half dead," so they had no excuse to pass him by. The hearers would not be likely to identify with these two people and their merciless conduct. But neither would they be inclined to identify with the victim who was beaten up. The buildup of suspense focuses on who the next person coming down the road is going to be. Given the values of the Jewish society of the time, it has to be an Israelite layperson who will appear in the role of hero and bind up the wounds of the injured man. Then the hearers can all go home reinforced in their cultural mindsets.

The plot is designed to encourage the expectation of an Israelite savior. But who shows up coming down the road? A Samaritan, the mortal enemy of the Jewish nation and religion.

To get an idea of how shocking this reversal of expectations would be for the original hearers, you may recall a movie entitled *Guess Who's Coming to Dinner?* In this film one of the principals is an editor of a liberal newspaper and a vigorous promoter of civil rights. His wife is in complete sympathy with his liberal views. They have a beautiful daughter upon whom they both dote and who dotes on them. One day the daughter announces that she has met a marvelous young man and that they have just become engaged. She expatiates loud and long on how much he is in full accord with all the social issues to which her father and mother are devoted. The parents are excited and say, "Well, bring him to dinner! We want to meet him!"

When the appointed day arrives and the engaged couple come to the door, the daughter rushes in first and embraces her beloved parents exclaiming, "I just can't wait till you meet him!" The audience has been built up to the same high pitch of expectancy to which the hearers of the parable were led before the appearance of the Samaritan. In this case, the parents are expecting a wonderful new addition to the family, one who will support their intense social concerns and projects. As the camera focuses on the entrance, in strides a tall, strapping, handsome black man, all smiles and ready to plunge into the arms of his prospective in-laws.

The camera then switches to the parents. We see the delighted expression on their faces fade with the suddenness of night descending in a deep canyon. The event has triggered something very unsettling for them. It is clear that on the conscious level they are very concerned about civil rights and social issues, but on the unconscious level their emotional values are being suddenly and severely confronted. This scene immediately raises the question, Just how open are they to equality with the black race? Clearly not to the point of welcoming a Black man into the family. Their own identification and emotional investment in the values engendered in them by their cultural conditioning has been hidden from them until now. On the conscious level they are all for civil rights. On the unconscious level they are not prepared to accept the possibility of cross-cultural grandchildren. The moment of truth having arrived, they react with horror. From the perspective of their deepest emotional values, the young man represents monumental corruption. The unexpected often shows us what our secret values really are.

To return to the parable of the good Samaritan, the hearers of Jesus' story are eagerly waiting to see who the next traveler is going to be on the road to Jericho. The clever design of the narrative has eased them into the expectation that it will be an Israelite layperson, on the lowest rung on the social ladder but still one of their own and hence acceptable. To their horror, the next traveler turns out to be a Samaritan! After the shock their first thought is, "He will surely finish off the poor guy!"

The Samaritan, however, starts ministering to the wounded man, pouring oil and wine into his wounds. He takes the injured man to an inn and pays for his stay. There the story ends, leaving the hearers without anybody in the story with whom to identify. They cannot identify with the priest, the Levite, or the victim, and it is inconceivable for most of them to identify with the Samaritan. That would be to accept the compassion and service of their mortal enemy. An impossible choice! For these hearers, the story must simply be untrue or makes no sense.

The message that is being communicated in this parable is that the kingdom of God knows no political or religious boundaries. The old maps of Israelite society are not relevant in this new kingdom. In the kingdom that Jesus is preaching, there are no rigid barriers between insiders and outsiders. More striking still, the temple in Jerusalem, center of the sacred in the popular mind, is no longer the sole criterion for holiness. In the person of the good Samaritan, the former —

universally accepted and unquestioned social and religious boundaries — all are swept away.

A favorite practice of the ancient Mediterranean cultures was to set up criteria for deciding who was in and who was out. In the kingdom revealed by Jesus, there is no way of deciding who is an insider and who is an outsider. This teaching must have sounded incredible for the people of that time who knew no other categories of judgment than the accepted social and religious distinctions. The great insight of early Christianity was that the kingdom of God is open to everyone. As Paul stated it, "There is no longer any distinction between Jew and Gentile, slave or free, male or female."

The movie described earlier is a modern parable dealing with basically the same issue. The implications of Jesus' teachings are especially apt in our time, because humanity is moving toward a global society with interaction among peoples in every conceivable way: economic, social, political, religious. The interiorization of Jesus' teaching about the unity of the human family as the most urgent expression of the will of God, must upstage every other value and consideration. Otherwise, violence, denial, and hypocrisy will abound.

The Samaritan in the parable was not rewarded. The kingdom of God is manifested in showing love whether or not it is accepted or its compassion appreciated. Divine love is its own reward. It is also irresistible. It keeps flowing until it finds someone who will receive it.

Would the first hearers of Jesus ever have understood the kingdom of God unless the one who came down the road was a Samaritan instead of the expected Israelite? And will we ever overcome our various forms of denial unless we are confronted by opposition or tragedy? The kingdom of God may be most active in what is most unacceptable to us, such as the dark side of our personality and the humiliation of acknowledging our mixed motivation at work even in our best intentions and in the service of others. Grace brings us to an ever-increasing awareness that under certain circumstances, we are capable of every evil. If the circumstances of our lives were challenged by starvation, serious illness, or a certain level of competition for money, prestige, position, love, or power, what would we actually do?

The Samaritan represents what we identify as monumental corruption. Our unquestioned values are profoundly undermined. We are forced to acknowledge the goodness of those we detest or distrust — perhaps even to accept compassionate service from them. The kingdom of God seeks to enter our lives just as they are. God wants us to show mercy, to take down doors, windows, and useless barriers of every kind. This is the message of the Samaritan, of the person or event that appears to us to be unmitigated evil — the master disguise in which God enters our lives in the fullest possible manner.

Jesus' parables leave the hearers with unresolved questions. The parable of the good Samaritan asks the question, "What is your idea of the kingdom of God?" Jesus' idea of the kingdom did not match the popular one of his time. In his view, the social map of first-century Palestinian culture is no longer a suitable vehicle for transmitting the kingdom of God.

Where does that leave the hearer? Perhaps with the question, "Do I want to live in this kingdom?"

To enter into the kingdom of God is to move beyond social expectations. Jesus identifies the action of the kingdom with the compassion of the Samaritan. The fact that the Samaritan is not converted suggests that the kingdom is not limited to religious attitudes or mindsets. Moreover, our supposed enemy may turn out to be our greatest benefactor.

According to this parable the kingdom of God has no fixed social, ethnic, racial, nationalistic, economic, or religious boundaries. There are no insiders or outsiders, no elite or nonelite. The abba whom Jesus reveals is the God of the human race as a family. Everyone must be concerned about everyone else. Unconditional love is the name of the game.

2

THE PARABLE OF
THE PUBLICAN AND THE PHARISEE

*"Two people went up to the temple to pray, one a Pharisee
and the other a tax collector. The Pharisee, standing by himself, was praying thus, 'God, I thank you that I am not like
other people: thieves, rogues, adulterers, or even like this tax
collector. I fast twice a week; I give a tenth of all my income.'
But the tax collector, standing far off, would not even look
up to heaven, but was beating his breast and saying, 'God, be
merciful to me, a sinner!' I tell you, this man went down to
his home justified rather than the other." (Luke 18:10–14a)*

The parable of the publican and the Pharisee reinforces
one of the central themes of the parable of the good Samaritan. The coming of the good Samaritan down the road to
Jericho signals the end of the social landscape and map of the
kingdom of God as perceived by Jesus' contemporaries. This
point is somewhat obscured by the manner in which Luke
introduces and concludes this parable in his gospel. He pre-
disposes the reader to look upon the pharisee as prideful. In
fact, the pharisee only did what the temple map required of
those who were considered insiders and members of the religious elite of the time. In fact, the social context of the temple,

as we now know it from other historical documents, would depict him as the ideal pious Pharisee! His speech is repeated almost word for word in other examples we have of pious prayers from the same period. His conduct and prayers are typical of the devout Pharisee.

The same map determining the proper conduct of one belonging to the sacred precincts of the temple as an insider also determines the place, the stance, and prayer of the publican (tax collector). He belongs to the group outside the bounds of the temple. He stands apart because he knows such is his proper place as an outsider. The place that he took was not a manifestation of his humility, as Luke hints, but simply of his awareness of his proper place as a sinner.

Thus the two men described in the parable manifest their relative places and status in the accepted culture of the time. One belongs to the sacred precincts of the temple and is an insider. The other belongs to the secular world and is an outsider. The social map calls for him to pray apart from the Pharisee who represents the holy. Thus from the text there is no evidence of merit or blame in the conduct or prayers of the two men.

The storyteller stuns the hearers with his conclusion: "The publican went home to his house (to the secular world) justified. The other man did not." These words come like a peal of thunder to the crowd. Luke attributes this statement to the humility of the publican and to the pride of the Pharisee, but the publican did not even make restitution for his extortions as Zacchaeus did (Luke 19:1–9) and the Pharisee thanked God for his good deeds, as was customary in the prayers of a devout Pharisee of his time.

Thus the main point of the parable emerges with stark clarity. The social map of the time is being abandoned and the kingdom of God is no longer to be found in the temple. The holy is outside and the unholy is inside. The activity of the kingdom of God has moved from the sacred precincts of the temple to the profane arena of the secular world. The Pharisee represents well the piety of the temple. The publican represents well the secular world. The sacred place is no longer the place of the sacred. The sacred has moved to everyday life.

3

THE PARABLE OF
THE PRODIGAL SON

"There was a man who had two sons. The younger of them said to his father, 'Father give me the share of his property that will belong to me.' So he divided the property between them. A few days later the younger son gathered all he had and traveled to a distant country, and there he squandered his property in dissolute living. When he had spent everything, a severe famine took place throughout that country, and he began to be in need. So he went and hired himself out to one of the citizens of that country, who sent him to his fields to feed the pigs. He would gladly have filled himself with the pods that the pigs were eating; and no one gave him anything. But when he came to himself he said, 'How many of my father's hired hands have bread enough and to spare, but here I am dying of hunger! I will get up and go to my father, and I will say to him, "Father, I have sinned against heaven and before you; I am no longer worthy to be called your son, treat me like one of your hired hands." ' So he set off and went to his father. But while he was still a far off, his father saw him and was filled with compassion; he ran and put his arms around him and kissed him. Then the son said to him, 'Father, I have sinned against heaven and before you; I no longer worthy to

be called your son.' But the father said to his slaves, 'Quickly, bring out a robe — the best one — and put it on him; put a ring on his finger and sandals on his feet. And get the fatted calf and kill it, and let us eat and celebrate; for this son of mine was dead and is alive again; he was lost and is found.' And they began to celebrate.

"Now his elder son was in the field; and when he came and approached the house, he heard music and dancing. He called one of the slaves and asked what was going on. He replied, 'Your brother has come, and your father has killed the fatted calf because he has got him back safe and sound.' Then he became angry and refused to go in. His father came out and began to plead with him. But he answered his father, 'Listen! For all these years I have been working like a slave for you, and I have never disobeyed your command; yet you have never given me even a young goat so that I might celebrate with my friends. But when this son of yours came back, who has devoured your property with prostitutes, you killed the fatted calf for him!' Then the father said to him, 'Son, you are always with me, and all that is mine is yours. But we had to celebrate and rejoice, because this brother of yours was dead and has come to life; he was lost and has been found.' "

(Luke 15:11–32)

This parable takes place in the context of a society where everyone was assigned a fixed place in the class structure. In that society a father was the representative of the law. The inheritance was of extreme importance and was governed by a legal code and maintained by strict rules. The father's role was to protect both the honor of the family and the inheritance. The inheritance could be divided prior to his death, but in this case it was the duty of the sons to set aside adequate funds to take care of him in his old age.

The story begins with the outrageous conduct of the younger son who demands his inheritance ahead of schedule and then, having received it, takes off for the good life. We hear about his progressive degradation. He finally winds up in disaster. A famine comes upon the country and he has nothing to eat. To avoid starving, he takes a job caring for pigs, an occupation that was considered apostasy from the Jewish religion. Eating pork was one of its religious taboos. In short, the prodigal hits bottom from every perspective.

The poverty of the prodigal is described in terms of a desperate lack of food. Nourishment belonged to the maternal function of this society, but there is no mother in the story. Maybe that was his problem. He is hungry and he recalls how well fed the servants were in his father's house. The thought comes, "I'll go back to my father's house. I won't ask to be his son. If only I can be one of the hired hands, I'll have something to eat."

He starts trudging back in his rags and smelling to high heaven of his charges in the pig sty. He has jeopardized the family's economic standing and put his father at risk by dissipating with foreigners that part of his inheritance that belonged by right to his father in his old age. Besides gross ingratitude, he has added the sin of injustice.

His father evidently has one eye on the road and is overwhelmed with boundless joy when he sees his ragamuffin son coming home. He dashes out and covers him with affectionate embraces and kisses. This free expression of love is totally out of character for a father in this patriarchal society. In the only other place in scripture where this term is used, Joseph "fell on his brothers' necks and kissed them affectionately" (Gen. 45:14–15).

Here, then, is a father who disregards his honor, the inheritance, and the patriarchal standards of the time, and acts like a mother. When the prodigal acknowledges his sin, the father does not even listen to his carefully prepared speech and the part about his becoming a hired hand. He immediately calls for the best robe, which is probably one of his own. He orders the servants to put sandals on his son's feet, a symbol of his full restoration to honor in the family. There is not the slightest questioning of his sincerity. Then the father calls for the fatted calf, and the music and dancing begin.

The elder son now appears. He has been faithfully serving his father on the land and working diligently for his share of the inheritance. The disappearance of the younger son has put his own share in jeopardy because now he is going to have to provide for his father's old age entirely out of his own resources. He has reason to be indignant at his younger brother and refers to him contemptuously as "that son of yours."

On the other hand, by refusing to go in to the party, the elder son sins against the fourth commandment, which requires him to honor his father. When his father graciously comes out to remonstrate with him, the elder son berates the old man for his goodness saying, "You have rewarded this son of yours who has not only wasted his share of the family fortune, but by living with prostitutes has risked the family blood line." Along with his offensive language, he dishonors both his father and his brother by refusing to take part in the celebration. Thus he has broken the legal code of the time just as much as the younger son, but in his own way.

This parable is obviously intended to subvert one of the favorite themes in the Old Testament — namely, that of the chosen and the rejected. Because of the older son's misconduct toward the father, the hearers are expecting the story of Jacob and Esau to be repeated. Jacob, the younger son, was chosen by God while Esau, the elder son, to whom the inheritance legally belonged, was rejected. The expectation is that the elder son in this story is also going to be rejected, and the hearers, who would have identified by now with the younger son, can rejoice along with him in being God's specially chosen people.

The conduct of the father, however, effectively destroys

the idea of Israel as the chosen people. Instead of rejecting the elder son for his disrespect, the father affirms, "You are always with me. Everything I have is yours." The elder son thus is assured of his share of the inheritance in spite of his misconduct. Just as the younger son is received back into the family in spite of dissipating his father's livelihood, so the elder son, who has just broken the fourth commandment by his insolent disrespect, is restored to favor. The father thus disregards the offenses of *both* sons. He puts completely aside his personal honor and the legal code. He shows himself equally disinterested in the immorality of his younger son and in the offensive self-righteousness that is the preoccupation of his elder son. Apparently the requirements of the Mosaic law are of no great importance to him. His conduct upstages both the misconduct of the younger son and the insistence on legal rights of the elder. The kingdom of God, it would seem from this parable, is not primarily concerned with conventional morality or legalities. The father acts, according to the accepted standards of that society, as a bad father. However, as Scott puts it, he turns out to be a very good mother. Clearly this father unites in himself the qualities of both mother and father. The father in this parable represents the abba whom Jesus reveals as the God of infinite concern and love for all his children — that is, for the whole human family.

What emerges as the primary concern of the father in this parable? It is to unite his two sons: to bring them together in love. Both are guilty of serious failings and he wants to forgive them both. This father's chief concern is not justice but mercy. The father communicates unconditional love to his two sons so that they in turn may show mercy to each other. According to Jesus, his heavenly Father is not especially interested in legal codes and in conventional morality. He seeks the unity of the human family, the removal of divisions and barriers, and the triumph of compassion by manifesting the maternal values symbolized in that culture by nourishment and overflowing affection.

The parable must have left the Jewish audience with their mouths open in astonishment. What they thought was their major claim to God's protection and love, his free election of them as his chosen people, is profoundly undermined by this parable. The fact is that everyone is chosen. This includes both public sinners, who know that they have offended God, and the self-righteous who deny their complicity in sin. This father forgives both but commands them to live together in peace and common concern — the kind of concern that the Father has shown in sending his Son into the world as the sign of his forgiveness of everything and everyone.

4

THE PARABLE OF LAZARUS AND THE RICH MAN

"There was a rich man who was dressed in purple and fine linen and who feasted sumptuously every day. And at his gate lay a poor man named Lazarus, covered with sores, who longed to satisfy his hunger with what fell from the rich man's table; even the dogs would come and lick his sores. The poor man died and was carried away by the angels to be with Abraham. The rich man also died and was buried. In Hades, where he was being tormented, he looked up and saw Abraham far away with Lazarus by his side. He called out, 'Father Abraham, have mercy on me, and send Lazarus to dip the tip of his finger in water and cool my tongue; for I am in agony in these flames.' But Abraham said, 'Child, remember that during your lifetime you received your good things, and Lazarus in like manner evil things; but now he is comforted here, and you are in agony. Besides all this, between you and us a great chasm has been fixed, so that those who might want to pass from here to you cannot do so, and no one can cross from there to us.'" (Luke 16:19–26)

In this parable, the sudden reversal of roles and expectations so characteristic of Jesus' teaching is once again

31

manifested. Two extreme situations are juxtaposed. A rich man dressed in purple, symbol of the upper classes and power, feasted not just well, but sumptuously — and not just on feast days, but every day. At the gate to his estate lay Lazarus the beggar. In the popular mindset of the time beggars were considered responsible for their miserable plight. Poverty was looked upon as a punishment for sin and for that reason, the hearers would be thinking, "It's his own fault."

Lazarus dies and is carried by angels to Abraham's bosom, symbol of the fulfillment of all the promises made by God to Israel. The rich man also dies and is buried in Hades. In Jewish religious literature, prior to this time, there is no mention of a chasm between the just and the unjust that extends beyond the grave. This is a new note that the parable here introduces. Abraham responds to the rich man's plea by pointing out that he had enjoyed every good thing during his earthly life and now is in torment, while the poor man had experienced just the opposite.

The kingdom of God in Jesus' preaching presupposes solidarity with the community and its needs. In this light we begin to see what was wrong with this rich man's behavior. No particular misdeeds of his are listed. The parable indicates that it was not his wealth that was the cause of his undoing but his use of it. He failed to share with the community the abundance that God had given him. Such is the true purpose of the blessings of wealth. Thus this parable inveighs against the sin of indifference that fails to share one's abundance with those in need. It does so by juxtaposing the rich man's private enjoyment of his great abundance with the extreme want of the beggar for whom no practical concern was offered.

The sin of the rich man could not have been his wealth as such, since Abraham too was a rich man and found favor with God as the book of Genesis attests. The rich man's fate suggests that his sin was his failure to pass through the gate of his estate and to respond to the desperate need of the beggar. The parable attacks the complacency of our divisions between rich and poor, the socially acceptable and the socially outcast. The gate symbolizes the grace that enables us to love our neighbor — everyone — as ourselves. The rich man stayed in his enclosure. His failure to go through the gate and to enter into solidarity with the one in need was the particular cause of his undoing.

Gates can be barriers or passageways into solidarity with others. In whatever way the rich man obtained his goods, whether through junk bonds or other means of getting rich quick, he failed to pass through the gate of his private interests and concerns to identify with someone whose situation was desperate and whom he could easily have helped. In the next life things will be reversed. If the rich man had gone through the gate to reach out to the beggar and had not simply used it as a barrier to protect himself and his property, his fate would have been quite different. God does not set up barriers. We do. Our relationship to our local community and to the human family as a whole determines whether we are in the kingdom or out of it, both now and in the next life.

To understand this teaching more clearly, let us look at a modern parable that seems to me to express in contemporary terms the main point of this parable. The classic movie, *Casablanca*, emphasizes what is meant by the word "solidarity" in this context. In the movie Rick, played by Humphrey Bogart, has a poignant romance with Ilsa, played by Ingrid Bergman, just before the German occupation of Paris in World War II. They agree to leave Paris on the last train. When she does not show up, his heart is broken. He has to leave to escape the Gestapo and winds up in Casablanca running a night club. Ilsa turns up one night at the night club with her husband who turns out to be the prime force in the underground of the French Resistance. Rick is completely undone by her reappearance in his life. After much misunderstanding she finally gets a chance to explain what happened. When they had met in Paris, she had believed that her husband had been killed. When he turned up unexpectedly, on the very day she and Rick were to leave Paris, she had decided that her husband who was sick and in hiding needed her and that her first duty was to him. Hence her decision not to meet Rick at the train. But now she confesses, "I loved you then and I still love you!" And a little later, "I ran away from you once. I cannot do it again."

The hero of the French Resistance is being tracked down by the Gestapo. Rick has possession of two visas. Ilsa finds herself in a double bind: to stay with Rick or to escape with her husband. She tells Rick, "You must decide for both of us." As the plot unfolds, he makes the painful decision to put her and her husband on the plane while he stays behind.

In making this choice, Rick does precisely what the rich man in the parable failed to do. He passes through the gate of his own little world into solidarity with the whole human family. He puts the desperate world situation of his time above his own happiness. He saw that the leader of the French Resistance, Ilsa's husband, was contributing to the undermining of Hitler's tyranny and that this heroic man needed the support of his wife in order to fulfill his role. He could have had Ilsa for himself, but he chose to let go of his private world with its alluring promise of personal happiness for the greater good of the whole human family. This is actually what God the Father has done according to the Christian faith, in sending his only begotten Son into the world to be crucified for our salvation. It is this insight into the heart of God and its manifestation in human affairs that makes this film so extraordinary.

As we saw in the parable of the prodigal son, the father throws away his honor and personal interests in order to enter into solidarity with his disobedient sons. The kingdom of God is for everyone who understands that solidarity with the human family, made concrete in our local community, is the name of the game. Truly marvelous is the gate that enables us to enter into communion with one another. In that communion the kingdom of God achieves its highest activity. We are empowered to be and to act like God. On the other hand, if we use the gate to protect ourselves from those in need, the gate becomes a barrier that may continue into the next life.

Both parables speak of human love that imitates divine love by joining the human family in its desperate needs. If we are rich, our wealth is for the community, not for us. And if we love, our love must take into account an ever-increasing identification with everyone in the human family.

The nature of the kingdom of God is that it has to be shared. Hence in the Christian perspective, community is the supreme value. To relate to the whole human family as God's family is the basic thrust of the gospel. That is why the refusal to be reconciled is such a serious matter and why, when Peter asked, "How many times must I forgive?" Jesus replied with a symbolic number meaning "without end." That is the proper way to love our neighbor as ourselves.

To be in the kingdom is to participate in God's solidarity with the poor by sharing with them the good things that have been given to us. In the New Testament the great sin is to be deaf to the cry of the poor whether that cry springs from emotional, material, or spiritual need. Although we cannot help but partake in some degree in social injustice because we live in this world, we must constantly reach out in concrete and practical ways to those in need. Divine love is not a feeling, but a choice. It is to show mercy. The rich man, although he saw the beggar starving at his doorstep and could easily have reached out to him, just went on eating, drinking, and reading his *Wall Street Journal*.

5

THE PARABLE OF
THE MUSTARD SEED

He said therefore, "What is the kingdom of God like? And to what shall I compare it? It is like a mustard seed that someone took and sowed in the garden; it grew and became a tree, and the birds of the air made nests in its branches."

(Luke 13:18–19)

The thrust of the parables is to subvert the distorted myths in which people live their lives. To understand what we mean by "living in a myth" just think of a couple of our own contemporary myths. Take the myth of "the All American Boy," for example. This is the young man who gets straight A's in college and graduate school, climbs the executive ladder, and perhaps becomes the head of a multinational. Or the "American Dream:" two cars in every garage, vacations in Florida, houses in Spain, and so forth. On a more serious level, the American dream has been a vision of America's invincibility, of its absolute entitlement in the eyes of God.

A myth is often what holds people's lives together. It is an attempt to resolve the tensions of everyday life by promising an idealized future in which one will be rescued from all the

36

problems of ordinary life. When a myth begins to falter, great leaders may try to find ways to recapture the glory of earlier days, like John F. Kennedy's effort to rekindle the American dream by sending a man to the moon. American astronauts did go to the moon, but meanwhile the Vietnam war devastated the prestige of American invincibility and with it the American dream.

For the Israelites of Jesus' time, the tension between everyday reality and a mythical vision of Israel as God's chosen people was felt with particular urgency. From the heyday of national power and prestige during the reigns of King David and King Solomon, Israel had been on a downhill slide for several centuries, its kingdom conquered and divided several times over. If one lives in occupied territories, as the Israelites of Jesus' time did, the question naturally arises, "Is this ghastly oppression by the Romans a punishment from God, or is our suffering just part of the human condition?" In the particular myth in which the people of first-century Israel were living, the kingdom of God had specific connotations of power, triumph, holiness, and goodness. The kingdom, when it came, would introduce a glorious new age of universal peace, with God's chosen people at the head of the nations.

The cultural symbol for this myth was the great cedar of Lebanon. Cedars of Lebanon were comparable to the huge redwood trees of California. They grew straight up for two or three hundred feet or more. Every kind of bird could enjoy their shade. This image was deeply embedded in the cultural conditioning of the Jewish people. The kingdom of God as a nation would be the greatest of all nations just as the great cedar of Lebanon was the greatest of all trees.

Instead, Jesus proposed this parable, "What is the kingdom of God really like? It is like a mustard seed" — proverbially the smallest and most insignificant of all seeds — "that someone took and sowed in his garden." For an alert hearer of Jesus' day, the detail about the garden would be a tip-off. In the Jewish view of the world, order was identified with holiness and disorder with uncleanness. Hence there were very strict rules about what could be planted in a household garden. The rabbinical law of diverse kinds ruled that one could not mix certain plants in the same garden. A mustard plant was forbidden in a household garden because it was fast spreading and would tend to invade the veggies. In stating that this man planted a mustard seed in his garden, the hearers are alerted to the fact that he was doing something illegal. An unclean image thus becomes the starting point for Jesus' vision of the kingdom of God in this parable.

If the starting point is an unclean image, the rest of the parable becomes even more perplexing. What do we know about a mustard seed, botanically speaking? It is a common, fast-spreading plant, which grows to about four feet in height. It puts out a few branches, and with some stretch of the imagination, birds might build a few down-at-the-heel nests in its shade.

Steeped in their cultural images of the great cedar of Lebanon, the hearers would be expecting the mustard seed, Jesus' symbol of the kingdom, to grow into a mighty apocalyptic tree. Jesus' point is exactly the opposite. It just becomes a bush. Thus the image of the kingdom of God as a towering cedar of Lebanon is explicitly ridiculed. According to Jesus, the kingdom of God is like a mustard seed, which some man illegally planted in his garden. It became a shrub and a few birds nested in its modest branches. That's all. The parable subverts all the grandiose ideas about what the kingdom is going to be like when it finally arrives.

One of the most firmly held Israelite expectations was that the kingdom of God would manifest the final triumph of God in history. Its arrival, heralded by the long-awaited Messiah, would rescue Israel from its miserable subservience to the Roman Empire. It was a future kingdom, not one in the here-and-now. Jesus' parable implies that if we accept the God of everyday life, we can find God in everyday life. We do not have to wait for an apocalyptic deliverance. We do not have to wait for a grandiose liberation. The kingdom is available right now.

The parables, according to Scott, are like handles on the mystery of the kingdom, pointers suggesting both what it is and what it is not. We cannot fully understand the kingdom because it is a mystery that transcends any possibility of being contained in a concept. But by rotating the wisdom of Jesus' sayings in our mind's eye and with the help of the parables, we can at least get a glimpse of it.

A parable points to something we only gradually come to know as we absorb the teaching of Jesus. In this parable he intimates that God is not necessarily going to intervene in this world for the triumph of the just. He may not intervene in an apocalyptic manner to deliver Israel or bring about justice and peace. He has entrusted the latter to us. We are not to wait around for an apocalyptic intervention to do the job.

If we lead a holy life — as opposed to a merely respectable one — we are likely to lose most of our friends and relatives. We might get one or two of them to follow our example, but it is like the mustard seed. We may get a modest result, but it is not in the nature of a cedar of Lebanon. All we are likely to get is an inconspicuous shrub of which there are plenty of others all around in great variety. The mustard seed is just one step ahead of being an ordinary weed.

How are we to understand this deliberate use by Jesus of the unclean and insignificant as images of his kingdom? It suggests that God's greatest works are not done on a grandiose level. Not in cathedrals, big buildings, or large mausoleums. Cathedrals can become museums rather than sources of inspiration for the Christian community. The kingdom is in everyday life with its ups and downs, and above all, in its insignificance. Such is where most people actually live their lives. The kingdom is thus readily accessible to everybody.

The parable affirms that grace is like a mustard seed sown in us, the smallest of all seeds. It is growing, but it is not going to turn us into a cedar of Lebanon. We will be doing well if we become a modest shrub.

So hard was it for people of Jesus' time to get over their idea of the kingdom of God as a triumphant institution that even the evangelists tried to change it into something great anyway. In other words, the myth recaptured the parable. The parable was meant to change one's idea about the kingdom, but what happened was that the old mindset began to interpret the parable in a way that was consistent with its former mythical expectations. There are four versions of this parable in the Gospels, three in the synoptics and one in the Gospel of Thomas, a document recovered about fifty years ago in the Nag Hammadi Gnostic Collection, which many exegetes think is closer in some places to the original oral tradition. For Luke and Matthew, contrary to all botanical good sense, the mustard seed does turn into a tree. In Mark, it turns into the greatest of shrubs. In Thomas, it turns into a great branch so that a lot of birds can rest in its shade. All of these expectations are contrary to the facts. A mustard seed does not become a tree, the greatest of shrubs, or put forth a great branch, however much one may want it to. The oral tradition was evidently influenced by the old expectations of grandeur as people gradually slipped back into their former mindsets. They lost the radical thrust and the incredible freedom to which the parable called them. For us too, it is a threat to our preconceived ideas and mythical belief systems, and hence there is a strong tendency to resist its stark realism.

If we are looking for a great expansion of our particular religion, nation, ethnic group, social movement, or whatever, into some great visible organization that fills the earth, we are on the wrong track. This is not God's idea of success. Where are the mightiest works of the kingdom accomplished? In our attitudes and hence in secret. Where there is charity, there is God. Opportunities to work for the homeless, the starving, the aging, are all readily available. No one may notice our good deeds, including ourselves. The kingdom of God manifests itself in the modest changes in our attitudes and in the little improvements in our behavior that no one may notice, including ourselves. These are the mighty works of God, not great external accomplishments.

"To what shall I liken the kingdom of God?" Jesus asked. The kingdom is manifested in ordinary daily life and how we live it. Can we accept the God of everyday life? If we can, then we can enjoy the kingdom here and now, without having to wait for an apocalypse or someone to deliver us from our difficulties.

6

THE PARABLE OF THE LEAVEN – I

He told them another parable: "The kingdom of God is like yeast that a woman took and mixed in with three measures of flour until all of it was leavened." (Matthew 13:33)

If the kingdom of God is like leaven, Jesus' teaching is absolutely revolutionary. In the ancient Israelite world, leaven — today's yeast — was a symbol of corruption. Modern English usage has given it a positive sense — fermentation and new life. But for the people of Israel, leaven was the archetype of corruption. It symbolized the unholy, the profane, of everyday life. *Un*leavened bread was the proper symbol of the holy, the sacred, the feast. Why was leaven regarded as such a lively symbol of corruption? In ancient times leaven was made by placing a piece of bread in a dark, damp place until it rotted and stank.

In Jesus' one-sentence tale, a woman took leaven and put it in three measures of flour, an amount sufficient to feed about fifty people. This is the exact measurement that we hear about in other places in scripture. Abraham ordered his wife Sarah to make three measures of bread for his three angelic visitors at the Oaks of Mamre. Hannah made this offering when she presented Samuel in the temple. The amount is thus related to epiphanies of God in the

Old Testament. But the epiphany here is quite different; it is an epiphany of corruption. In this case, the leaven is kneaded into an enormous amount of dough and in due time the whole batch becomes leavened. Are we to understand that the kingdom of God is working like leaven in the dough to form a huge mass of corruption?

The hearers are naturally asking the question, "Is this man saying that good is evil?" Jesus' parables work not only through similarities, but, as Scott points out, through dissimilarities. The usual image of leaven as the symbol of corruption is used in this parable to emphasize the negative aspect — or what seems like the negative aspect — of the kingdom. For one thing, the parable questions the hearers' easy assumption of the predictability of what is good and what is evil. It confronts their preconceptions regarding where goodness is to be found. In this respect, it coheres with the parable of the good Samaritan where the boundaries of social stratification are dramatically subverted. The Samaritan, the Israelite's epitome of the bad guy, turns out to be a hero.

In this parable, an even more profound boundary is being challenged. Can evil be good? Recalling Jesus' custom of reaching out in table fellowship with the outcasts of society, the kingdom of God is revealed to be active in marginal people and in the marginalized. Where is the kingdom if it is not in the holy, the sacred, and the acceptable places? Jesus, by his example and preaching, says, "Look for it in the most unexpected places." According to the parables, the kingdom of God is free to appear anywhere, any time, and under any guise. It does not fit into our presuppositions or expectations, and still less, our demands. In fact, it deliberately removes, prop by prop, everything holding up our ideas of the nature of the kingdom and where it is to be found.

A story might help to grasp the shock value of this saying. An acquaintance of mine in California with a very active and ongoing practice of contemplative prayer, experienced terrible tragedy. Her only son, a young man just coming out of college with every promise for a brilliant future, was shot to death on the street for no reason at all by a sociopath, a man who just wanted to kill somebody for the sheer pleasure of the exercising absolute power over someone. The murderer was convicted and sent to prison. Of course, the mother was devastated by the senseless murder of her son. She was plagued by the harrowing questions: "Why couldn't God have done something to prevent it? Why did it have to be my son? Is this a punishment for my sins? Does God really love me?" For her, the tragedy was unmitigated evil, monumental corruption.

After much prayer she decided to write this man and tell him that she forgave him. For a year she received no response. Finally a very matter-of-fact letter came, acknowledging her letter but without the least sign of remorse. She wrote back asking if he would be willing to see her. Again a wait of about a year. Finally a note came saying yes. She drove the long distance to the prison, and accompanied by the social worker assigned to his case, she met the murderer of her son. He spent most of the time describing, absolutely deadpan, the horrendous childhood he had suffered. He was an unwanted child, continually subjected to physical abuse in the extreme. As a consequence, he had become totally antisocial and narcissistic. At one point in the conversation, he confessed, "You cannot imagine the immense joy I felt when I stood over your son and realized that I had killed him!" It was his moment of ultimate power. For the first time the sense of self-worth that had been systematically crushed by his whole previous life experience flooded over him to the point of ecstatic triumph.

The mother stood her ground. Her forgiveness was unshaken, and she reaffirmed it to him. The social worker was flabbergasted by the spirit of this woman who could calmly forgive the one who had caused her the greatest pain of her life. The social worker wrote to her sometime later saying, "This man has started to change. He shows a little more courtesy and consideration for the other inmates."

The woman felt moved to stay in contact with the prisoner. She offered to return. His immediate response was poignant: "Please don't come again. I'm afraid, if you keep coming, I'll have to face the unbearable pain of my childhood." His antisocial behavior had enabled him to maintain absolute denial of a past that was too painful to face up to. But she did go back. At the end of the interview, she embraced him.

I do not know what the final outcome of this exchange will be. She is still writing, still visiting him, still feeling the pain of her great loss. In her last interview, she detected as she gave him a farewell hug, a tiny tear in the corner of his eye. In a very real sense, she has become his mother and he is becoming her son.

Was God's kingdom active in the monumental corruption involved in this event? Perhaps the movement of one person from total inhumanity to the capacity to shed a single tear is a greater act of God than the sanctification of a saint? Who can judge? Jesus often identified himself with the outcasts of society that everybody had given up on by sharing a meal with them. Evidently the kingdom of God was active there. The kingdom, of course, is at work everywhere, but the parable suggests that it is mightiest in the marginalized and in events that we characterize as unmitigated evil. To draw a single tear, to us almost imperceptible, from a heart of stone must cause all creation to vibrate with joy and wonder at the power of the kingdom and of God's love.

7

THE PARABLE OF THE LEAVEN – II

He told them another parable: "The kingdom of God is like yeast which a woman took and mixed in with three measures of flour until all of it was leavened." (Matthew 13:33)

Jesus says the kingdom of God is like leaven. In the ancient Mediterranean world as we saw, leaven had very negative associations. It was the archetype of uncleanness and corruption. Leaven was made by putting a piece of bread in a dark, damp place until it molded and stank. Both leaven and the process of leavening were symbols of corruption.

In the Jewish tradition men were considered ritually pure and women were ritually unclean. As a consequence, rabbis were forbidden to speak to women in public. No rabbi giving a formal sermon would cite a woman as heroine of any story. Jesus frequently did so in his parables, however, ignoring the stereotypes of his day.

In this parable Jesus addresses the popular idea that the kingdom of God is holy, good, and triumphant. The kingdom turns out to be active in the marginalized and the poor, both of whom were regarded in Jesus' day as objects of God's abandonment. The state of poverty was regarded as the result of sin and hence was a symbol of corruption. Natural calamities were also regarded as punishments from God.

In this parable a woman takes leaven, the archetype of corruption, and hides it in three measures of flour, the same amount that Sarah used to make bread for the angels who visited Abraham at Mamre. There is thus the implication in the parable of a divine epiphany. Moreover, the enormous amount of dough that is leavened suggests not just ordinary corruption, but monumental corruption.

The hearers are surely thinking, "How can the kingdom of God, which is supposed to be holy, good, and triumphant, be like leaven, the archetype of corruption? Is the preacher implying that evil is good?"

Let me propose a story that seems to raise the same issues as this parable. The great popular art form of our time is the movies. Everybody goes to the movies nowadays. Once in a while one of them proposes similar questions to those that arise in the parables. Not long ago I saw a movie called *Our Sons*. It was about two mothers, with two gay sons. One of the mothers was a poor woman whose fundamentalist religious background caused her to regard her son's lifestyle as an absolute taboo; she had completely disassociated herself from him. The other woman was upper middle-class and a well-to-do liberal. She considered herself to have adjusted well to the situation. In fact, she was just as angry and resentful as the other mother, but in her own way. It was clear to her son that he was not accepted.

As the plot unfolds, the son of the poor woman is dying of AIDS and longs to see his mother once again, but is afraid to write to her. His friend persuades his own mother, as a special favor to him, to visit the poor woman and pay for her to travel to see her dying son. The poor mother turns out to be a down-to-earth woman who sees through the denial of the other mother. *Our Sons* might have been called "our growth." A growth process is clearly taking place in the two mothers as they struggle with their common humiliation. The behavior of the sons is an equal no-no for both of them, though each reacts in a different way.

Finally, when the poor woman comes to see her dying son, she makes several visits but each time she stays near the door. Something inside her remains fearful and unreconciled. The son is getting weaker and weaker as death approaches. When it is time for her to return to her home, she comes for a final visit and to say good-bye. This time she cautiously tiptoes over to his bed. The camera focuses on her hand as she ever-so-slowly and cautiously reaches out and touches her son's hand extended toward her. She has at last overcome her prejudices and fears.

The kingdom of God is active where we perceive monumental corruption. If the poor mother had not reached out and touched her son in a sign of reconciliation and forgiveness, what would have become of her? She would have remained permanently walled up in her own security system, desperately trying to protect herself from the pain of the reality of the situation and from the demands of true love.

The divine action makes use of what seems like corruption in our eyes to change us, to open us to the kingdom, which is present where we least expect it. The kingdom of God is present and available in what happens. The question is not why upsetting or devastating things happen, but what we are going to do with them now that they are happening? The divine compassion is intervening in our behalf, but not on the level we want it to be or can perceive it to be. It is working mightily at a deeper level where grace enables us to say yes to God in the events of daily life.

In reaching out to her son, the mother opened herself to God's salvation. By being reconciled with her son, she enabled him to die in peace. The kingdom of God manifests itself in solidarity with other people, in sympathy with their misfortune, and in unconditional love. It is most active in situations that seem to us to represent monumental corruption.

The Jewish religion of the time identified everyday life with corruption and the sacred with the temple rituals and the great feasts. Jesus teaches that everyday life is the place of the sacred. The temple is no longer the place to look for it. Everyday life is the arena where the kingdom is most powerful. The kingdom is especially present and active when we are confronting what we think is monumental corruption. What are we to do with it? Jesus does not give the answer in the parable; he just invites us to beware of predicting, on the basis of our prepackaged beliefs, what is good and what is evil.

8

THE PARABLE OF THE LEAVEN – III

He told them another parable: "The kingdom of God is like yeast that a woman took and mixed in with three measures of flour until all of it was leavened." (Matthew 13:33)

How can the kingdom be like leaven? The teaching of Jesus challenges our attempts to discern what is good or evil on the basis of the accepted norms of the sacred in our respective cultures. In the Israelite society, leavened bread represented the unholy, the everyday, while unleavened bread represented the sacred, the feast day. Jesus implies that the kingdom of God may appear under any guise including corruption. Thus Jesus ate with outcasts, sinners, and the marginalized. In fact, he ate more meals with them than with the religious authorities of his time. By sitting down to table with sinners, which in his culture was a statement of identification with their community, Jesus forfeited his own moral purity. Did that significant gesture mean that he approved of extortion, prostitution, and the various forms of misbehavior of public sinners? Obviously his table fellowship with them did not mean approval of sinful behavior. What his conduct did reveal was that reaching out in love, reconciliation, and forgiveness are vastly more important in God's eyes than moral incorruption.

What forms might monumental corruption take for us to-day? It could be an accident resulting in a serious physical or mental disability. It could be what we regard as moral reprobation in someone dear to us, as in the case of the two sons in the previous chapter, or it could be a problem in our own conscience. In the eyes of the beholder the situation looks like a disaster. In reality, it can be a great blessing, an opportunity for God to heal us at the deepest level.

An extraordinary example of monumental corruption of a physical kind is exemplified for me in the life of the daughter of one of our neighbors. This child was injured early in life and for the past twenty-two years has been completely help-less, requiring twenty-four hour a day care on the part of her parents. She cannot feed, dress, or do anything for herself. She just is. These parents have shown this child so much love and caring that she seems to enjoy a sense of complete secu-rity. When you look into the eyes of this girl, you have the sense of looking into the eyes of someone who has no fear; of one who because of the heroic devotion of her parents, has been able to remain a child all her life retaining all the delightful qualities of childhood. She cannot walk, speak, or move her body; but she looks at you with utter simplicity, and the depth of acceptance in her eyes is like looking into the eyes of God. The acceptance of the tragedy and their re-sponse to it has enabled her parents to connect with God's love in an extraordinary way.

In the light of this example, I venture to suggest that our attitude toward what we regard as monumental corruption has to be changed, not the corrupting situation itself. Our tendency of course is to want to change the painful or shame-ful situation right away. But some situations are designed to change us, and our acceptance of them marks the place where our personal redemption really begins.

This parable of the leaven sounds the same chord that will later reverberate fully in Jesus' own personal experience of monumental corruption. When God's Son dies on the cross, not a single angel or human comes to his aid. The Father of this Son, as far as external evidence goes, could not care less about what happens to him. Jesus is rejected by the civil and religious authorities and by his own people, and abandoned by his disciples. From the cross he witnesses his life and teaching destroyed before his eyes.

Our experience of abandonment, the seeming absence of God on the spiritual journey, together with our temptations and the tendency to moral failure that frightens us, may actually be a powerful manifestation of the kingdom, according to the extraordinary reversal of values that Jesus proposes as the path to perfect joy and freedom.

Few people have understood this teaching. Saint Francis of Assisi was one. There is a story in which a favorite disciple, Brother Leo, asks him what perfect happiness is. Saint Francis answers, "Suppose you arrive cold and hungry at the gate of a monastery on a snowy night, and the porter slams the door in your face. Standing in the snow, shivering, you plead for mercy. He comes out and beats you with a stick. Ah! Brother Leo, that is perfect happiness!"

The kingdom of God does not operate on the level of appearances, and rarely on the level of signs and wonders, but God's apparent absence in daily life does not mean that the divine intervention is not present. On the contrary, it is present in a very real but hidden way. The kingdom manifests its incomparable power by changing our inner dispositions and attitudes. There may be no great deliverance, no sensational conversion; just small changes for the better in the way we react to the same old routines and our customary failures.

God is not limited by our ideas of where the kingdom may or may not be functioning. As we saw in the parable of the Pharisee and the publican, it is clearly not limited to sacred places. It is focused in everyday life. More precisely, it is present in the apparent corrupting situations of every-day life. Indeed, the parable implies that the power of the kingdom is more active there than anywhere else.

God reserves the right to appear under any guise. But because our self-centeredness is so deeply ingrained, it may take monumental corruption of some kind for us to begin to question our attitudes and motivation. These are what have to be changed, not necessarily the situation.

Who is this God whose chief command is that we forgive and show love for one another? If God loves us infinitely, God must be totally involved in our moral melodrama. We believe, in fact, that God has taken upon and into Godself in the person of Jesus Christ, all our sinfulness — that is, our whole experience of monumental corruption in ourselves and its consequences in our lives. In other words, God expects us to go on trusting God implicitly even in the face of our own monumental moral corruption. In a poem by Thomas Merton, the question is raised, "Who is God?" The response is, "Mercy, within mercy, within mercy."

9

THE PARABLE OF THE LEAVEN – IV

He told them another parable: "The kingdom of God is like yeast which a woman took and mixed in with three measures of flour until all of it was leavened." (Matthew 13:33)

It is characteristic of the parables to ask the question, "What makes you think that the world is the way you see it?"

In the minds of the Jewish hearers of the time, the kingdom of God had certain connotations suggesting the ultimate triumph of God in the world. The kingdom as Jesus sees it turns out to be quite different. The life and death of Jesus, in which God does not intervene, indicates that the kingdom of God is not to be found in miraculous occurrences, in being rescued from the inevitable results of our stupidity and misdeeds, in having all our needs amply provided for, or even in overcoming our sins, but rather in living our lives in union with God.

According to the parables, God is in complete solidarity with the outcasts of society. Escape into an ideal kind of lifestyle or rescue from life's difficulties and problems are both rejected by Jesus as solutions to the problems of living

54

in this world. The solution is not in getting away from our problems, but in realizing that God is totally present and supporting us in them. The most striking example of this is that God does not destroy death, but joins us in death. Our expectations of becoming paragons of piety, great contemplatives, attaining higher stages of consciousness — all subtly aimed at carrying us beyond the daily troubles of ordinary life — are not the way into the kingdom. Rather, the kingdom consists in finding God *in* our disappointments, failures, problems, and even in our inability to rid ourselves of our vices.

I joined the Trappists in 1944, long before the reforms of the Second Vatican Council. After having lived a strict monastic life for six years, in which I followed all the rules, appeared at all the spiritual exercises, never overslept or overate, wore the religious habit all the time including to bed, tried not to judge those who did not keep the rule as well as I did, rarely spoke to anybody except the abbot and novice master, worked hard, wrote home only once or twice a year, rarely had a visit from relatives and friends — in short, after I had faithfully practiced all the austerities of the Trappist Order, the monastery burned down. I was breathing smoke as I came down the stairway from the dormitory to the guesthouse — there was no other means of escape — into the source of the fire. The building was a fire trap from the word go. If it had not been for someone calling, "Stay close to the floor and come this way," I would have died of smoke inhalation. I leapt out a first-floor window and landed in a snowbank. It was then that the insight came to me: "Maybe God isn't as interested in this highly structured lifestyle as I am!"

It took another twenty years to work that insight into my monastic vision. It is hard for any insight to penetrate a mindset that is profoundly culturally conditioned, which is certainly the case in any form of strict religious training.

It may take disappointment, tragedy, illness, loss of friends, and near death experiences to shake us free.

The parables perform a similar service. They suggest that our idea of the kingdom may not be the correct one. Our ideas of God and the kingdom need to be expanded and to grow continuously. God is just as present in human relationships and in nature as in religious services. While religious rituals certainly have significant value, they are not to be identified with the kingdom. For the kingdom of God is in internal attitudes rather than in external observances. According to the parable of the Pharisee and the publican, the kingdom of God is more available in everyday life, with its routines, failures, disappointments, joys, and successes than in sacred places, shrines, and rituals. It becomes present to us and in us by our consent and by the dispositions that the Holy Spirit instills within us, the chief of which is faith that God is truly and secretly intervening to heal us despite any and all appearances to the contrary.

Was God present to Jesus when he abandoned him on the cross? Is he with us as we struggle with tragedy or with impossible situations? Apocalyptic myths look for a savior to resolve all problems. But to resolve all problems is to miss the point. The kingdom is manifested by our attitude toward our problems, not by their disappearance. That is how Jesus sanctifies the outcasts and whatever is outcast in us.

What idea of the kingdom begins to emerge as we listen attentively to the parable of the leaven? It is that the leaven, moral corruption, is not always replaced by the unleavened bread, the symbol of the holy; that daily problems are not normally changed by any divine intervention that we can see or feel. Hope is the grace that trusts God in the midst of everydayness with its ever-recurring trips to nowhere and the recycling of the same old temptations. We are left with the hope of transformation, but without any experience of it happening.

10

THE PARABLE OF
THE BARREN FIG TREE

"A man had a fig tree planted in his vineyard; and he came looking for fruit on it and found none. So he said to the gardener, 'See here! For three years I have come looking for fruit on this fig tree, and still I find none. Cut it down! Why should it be wasting the soil?' He replied, 'Sir, let it alone for one more year, until I dig around it and put some manure on it. If it bears fruit next year, well and good; but if not, you can cut it down.'" (Luke 13:6–9)

The parable of the barren fig tree recalls the recurrent theme in the Old Testament of the barren made fruitful by the Lord's direct intervention. The birth of John the Baptist is the classic example. His mother by the power of God became fertile in her old age, and to the astonishment of everyone, brought forth the child who would become the greatest of the prophets. Rachel, the beloved of Isaac, like Sarah, the wife of Abraham, was also barren until she was made fruitful by God.

The expectation of the original hearers of this parable, then, would be that God will intervene and turn this wretched tree, that has not produced any fruit for three years, into a flourishing tree bearing a superabundance of figs. In the Old Testament, the fig tree was the symbol of God's blessing and special love for God's people.

The gardener suggests putting some manure around the ailing plant. A delicate touch! The text uses a more refined word, "manure," but the actual meaning is closer to "dung." Hardly a decorous word in religious discourse, but Jesus did not hesitate to use it. It adds a certain earthiness — if not outright pungency — to the story.

What are we left with at the conclusion of this parable? A tree that is good for nothing. The gardener offers to shovel manure around it, but there is no indication that any new growth will actually occur. This tree and its predicament are striking symbols of daily life, especially when our efforts to do good fail or seem to be fruitless, our prayer periods are as dry as dust, and nothing ever happens. In addition, there is no sense of God's presence in daily life, no enlightenment experience, while our faults continue, people blame us unjustly, and disappointments multiply. Our spiritual life seems to be dead. What are we to do? The parable seems to say, just keep waiting.

This parable hints that it does not matter if we do not succeed in our own estimation or in that of others. The divine presence is so present that nothing can take it from us. Of course, we can still reject God, but someone who is seeking God is not about to do that. When we realize the fact of God's closeness, success and failure are relativized. We simply do what we can: that is, we throw a little manure — symbol of our fruitless efforts — on the old stick. Of course it is not going to grow, because it is dead. But in some mysterious way, because of God's solidarity with us in everyday life, something much more important happens.

This parable addresses something very deep in human nature and in the best of people. It is the perplexing question, "Why, when I do my best to pray, to do good, and to try to get closer to God, make sacrifices for others and put up with all kinds of trials, am I so beset with troubles, break an arm or a leg, turn up with some debilitating disease, lose a loved one, go through a painful divorce, live at the edge of financial ruin, or fall into some grievous addiction?" In other words, "Are life's reverses signs of God's punishment for my moral lapses, or are they just tests of my patience? Can I hope that God will eventually reward me with some high state of perfection or rescue me from our troubles by means of some apocalyptic deliverance?"

The parable suggests that Jesus does not recommend that we count on either expectation. Meanwhile, we reach out desperately for something to lean on in the face of difficulties, reverses, and heartbreaks.

In the light of the parables, it is a mistake to aim at a mystical state that we can feel, understand, and enjoy, all of which easily give rise to the temptation to feel superior to others. Jesus nowhere represents mystical union as the goal of the kingdom — still less, the prayer of quiet or the prayer of union. And less still, various supernatural interventions such as locutions, ecstasies, visions, charismatic gifts, and spiritual highs. These all feed into the naive idea that the kingdom of God will solve all problems, put "me" in a place beyond the everyday, the normal, and the nitty-gritty — in short, that the purpose of the kingdom of God is to make "me" feel special. We *are* special, but not because of those things. What is special about us is God's incredible solidarity with our ordinary lives: with our sense of failure, futility, getting nowhere spiritually, and our lack of inner resources to cope with our particular difficulties. In the parables daily life is so clearly the place where the kingdom is working that symbols of success are totally irrelevant. They are like icing on a cake. We cannot live on icing. We need more substantial food. Trust in God disregards the evidence of everyday life that God is absent or forgetful of us and brings us into direct contact with the God of everyday. The God of pure faith is so close: closer than breathing, closer than thinking, closer than choosing, closer than consciousness itself.

An enlightened faith seems very ordinary. One might scarcely notice it. It accepts the way things are and finds God vibrantly present in the most insignificant situations and in the most unexpected disguises. "Dung" in this parable is the symbol of humble hope, which keeps trusting in God without trying to analyze or resolve the tension between the hard realities of everyday life and God's sovereignty.

In a world in which God seems to be absent, people have to conjure up ideal situations in order to help themselves survive. And so poets and seers elaborate myths, one of which for religious people at least is to pass into a world of moral perfection, wisdom, and bliss; the other is to await the apocalyptic vindication of one's nation, race, ethnic group, religion, or bedraggled reputation.

Does the death and resurrection of Jesus offer a new myth into which we can escape by moving into an idealized state of perfection or into some apocalyptic deliverance? Not according to the parables. And not according to the crucifixion narratives of the synoptic Gospels in which Jesus' abandonment by the Father — "My God, my God, why have you forsaken me?" — seems to question his very identity as the Son of God.

The divine emptiness of Jesus is the point at which the power and mercy of the kingdom are maximized. We experience the same divine emptiness in our daily lives as we wait for something to happen that will fix everything that seems wrong in our particular environment or in us. Jesus in the parables affirms, "The kingdom is right where you are with your bundle of difficulties, your sense of getting nowhere and waiting in prayer for experiences that never happen." Divine union is not the achievement of some perfection of our own or an escape from our external problems, but is the radical change of attitude that enables us to deal effectively with our weaknesses and our problems — the humble acceptance of our lives just as they are, including the monumental moral corruption we may find in ourselves.

This experience of failure can cause no little disappointment and disillusionment. But disappointment in *what* is the question we have to ask. The answer is usually to be found in our deep-seated expectations, of course. Divine love is not normally going to change the situation by some great miracle. It is trying to change us, so that we can courageously and lovingly unite ourselves to God in the situation.

It is a mistake, then, to look for spiritual experiences in contemplative prayer or to judge our progress by them. The essence of contemplative prayer is not spiritual experience, but the purification of the unconscious. That process, usually quite lengthy, is what radically changes our attitudes and enables us to see ourselves as we truly are. Contemplation must not be presented as a road to glory. It is easy to become attached to spiritual experiences. The regular practice of contemplative prayer initiates the purification of the unconscious with all its repressed emotional pain: anger, shame, grief, fear, discouragement. Our experience, therefore, is not likely to be of an abundant harvest of delicious figs, but rather of "the dung."

Gardening is the first job that Adam was given in the garden of Eden; it is the symbol of what everybody's job is: shoveling manure to make the unfruitful fig tree (us) bloom. It will never bloom because of the manure, but God, touched by our persevering efforts and patient endurance, may make the thing blossom anyway — not because of our efforts and patience, but because of God's most tender love for us.

What happens to the barren fig tree if there is no one, like this concerned gardener, to take an interest in it and to try to save it?

11

THE PARABLE OF THE LOST COIN

"What woman having ten silver coins, if she loses one of them, does not light a lamp, and search carefully until she finds it? When she has found it, she calls together her friends and neighbors, saying, 'Rejoice with me, for I have found the coin that I had lost.'" (Luke 15:8–9)

This parable is not unlike the parable of the mustard seed. In that parable the Lord seems to be burlesquing the popular expectations of the kingdom as a giant cedar of Lebanon. As if Jesus were to say, "You are looking for a cedar of Lebanon, the great apocalyptic tree, and all I am asking of you is to become an insignificant little shrub."

If we can imagine the astonished faces of the hearers, it is not hard to picture Jesus' amusement at the collapsing of their house of cards. This parable continues in a similar vein.

A certain woman has lost a coin. A drachma was about the same as a denarius, one day's wage for a common laborer. It was not a lot of money. But she is looking everywhere for this coin, sweeping the house up and down. Some of the hearers are now getting excited and want to help her. When she finally finds it, there is great joy! She calls friends and neighbors, and they rejoice over her recovery of the tiny sum.

Jesus once again juxtaposes the grandiose expectations in the popular mind regarding how the kingdom is expected to appear in our lives, and how it actually appears. The woman finally finds the coin of modest value. That is the extent of God's intervention. Thus the kingdom is identified with the ordinary. She did not win the state lottery. Jesus undermines grandiose expectations of all kinds . For one reason: they are not likely to happen.

In the three parables that appear in chapter fifteen of Luke — the prodigal son, the lost sheep, and the lost coin — Luke seems to be intent on justifying Jesus' conduct in eating and drinking with public sinners. In his view, Jesus' purpose is to call them to repentance. In fact, the original meaning of the texts according to contemporary exegetes has little to do with repentance but focuses rather on the nature of the kingdom.

In the Gospel of Thomas a number of the parables are found in a different form from that reported in the synoptic Gospels. There is one parable that appears only in Thomas. Many exegetes think it is genuine because it follows the patterns that are familiar in Jesus' parables: shock value, an undermining of grandiose ideas about the kingdom, and identification of the kingdom with the unclean, the marginalized, and the outcasts of society.

The parable reminds us of the story of the widow of Zarephath in 1 Kings 17:8–15. There was a great famine in her country. The prophet Elijah, in desperate hunger, asked the widow for a morsel of bread and she replied that she had nothing to give him. The prophet then miraculously filled her empty jar saying, "The jar of meal shall not be spent, nor the cruze of oil, until the day that the Lord sends rain upon the earth."

The parable in the Gospel of Thomas has a different ending:

The kingdom of God is like a certain woman who was carrying a jar full of meal. While she was walking on a road still some distance from home, the handle of the jar broke and the meal emptied out behind her on the road. She did not realize it. She had noticed no accident. When she reached her house she set the jar down and found it was empty. (Thomas 97)

This story tells us that the kingdom of God is present in failure, accident, and emptiness. In her case, there was no prophet to come to her rescue, no visible divine intervention. There was just accident, failure, everydayness, the ordinary. The teaching of Jesus is that those are precisely the situations where the miraculous activity of the kingdom takes place. This means that the kingdom must be active at a deeper level than we are normally looking for or expecting. Nowhere does Jesus say there is *no* divine intervention. It is just not on the level that we would like it to be. In this remarkable parable, the divine intervention is represented by the empty jar.

This raises the question, "Is God just as present in absence as in presence?" Or to put it another way, "Is the divine intervention always there supporting us whether we think it is present or not?"

The answer of the parables is emphatically yes. The kingdom of God is active in failure, ordinariness, everydayness. If we wait for a miraculous rescue, a vindictive triumph, or for some idealized lifestyle to appear, we are looking for the wrong kingdom, certainly not the one that Jesus is revealing.

There is no place to go to find the kingdom because it is always close at hand. We do not need to look for success because the kingdom is equally present in failure. What is disconcerting for the hearers in both of these parables is that the kingdom is not only present and active in failure and in ordinariness, but is at work in the unclean, in the prostitutes and tax collectors to whom Jesus extends table fellowship.

According to Jesus, God is in total solidarity with ordinary daily life with its poignant failures in the spiritual journey as well as in everything else. Thus God's mercy invites us to show compassion and solidarity with all the other sinners in the world, including public sinners and street people, who in the parable of the great dinner, are the only ones who finally got in (Luke 14:16–24).

The kingdom is present not in grandiose accomplishments, but in showing practical love in humble ways, day after day, and in refusing to allow our failures and disappointments to hide God's love from us. God invites us to share the divine emptiness. The divine emptiness might also be described as total vulnerability: the willingness to be hurt over and over again without loving less but more. That means never giving up on anyone, not even on ourselves. Of such is the kingdom of God.

12

THE PARABLE OF THE GREAT DINNER

*"Someone gave a great dinner and invited many. At the time
for dinner he sent his slave to say to those who had been invited, 'Come, for everything is ready now.' But they all alike
began to make excuses. The first said to him, 'I have bought a
piece of land, and I must go out and see it; please accept my
regrets.' Another said, 'I have bought five yoke of oxen, and I
am going to try them out; please accept my regrets.' Another
said, 'I have just been married and therefore I cannot come.'
So the slave returned and reported this to his master. Then the
owner of the house became angry and said to his slave, 'Go
out at once into the streets and lanes of the town and bring
in the poor, crippled, the blind, and the lame.' And the slave
said, 'Sir, what you have ordered has been done, and there is
still room.' Then the master said to the slave, 'Go out to the
roads and lanes, and compel people to come in, so that my
house may be filled.'" (Luke 14:16b–23)*

There are three accounts of this parable: one from Matthew, one from Luke, and one from the Gospel of Thomas.
In Matthew's Gospel, the householder becomes a king. It is
part of Matthew's allegory that those who do not come to
this party will get the cold shoulder in the future. In Luke

the householder takes revenge on those who insulted him by refusing his invitation. In all these versions, the great dinner is the symbol of the kingdom of God. Those who come to the meal receive salvation, and those who decline are rejected.

Why do all three traditional accounts make such a big deal about those who decline? For one thing, they all offer rather lengthy excuses, all of which are somewhat lame. In a village culture, one's honor was all-important and depended on one's acceptance by one's peers. Attendance at an important dinner party was one such symbol of acceptance. All those originally invited lived in houses and hence belonged to the upper classes. Since the first two invitations failed, the expectation of the hearers is that the third will be accepted. In the parable of the good Samaritan, the first two travelers pass by and the third turns out to be merciful. In the parable of the talents, the first two servants are well received and the third is rejected.

The fact that in this parable all three invitations are refused, emphasizes the total rejection of the householder and the utter shame that he suffers from his peers. The disgrace of the householder seems to have caused the three versions of the parable to lose something of their original force. The evangelists provide opportunities for the householder to regain his honor (if not to get his revenge) by rejecting the original invitees. The dinner, however, continues to represent the messianic banquet prophesied by Isaiah.

As the parable unfolds in Luke, when the householder is rejected by all his well-to-do peers in the village, he flies into a rage and orders his servants to go into the streets and bring in the lame, the blind, and the disabled. The invitation to the disabled suggests to the hearers of the time that the feast is a symbol of the messianic kingdom when all those who have been oppressed by diseases or by Israel's enemies will at last be raised up to an exalted stature and Israel's honor will be restored.

In the parable of the mustard seed, the hearers expected the seed to grow into a cedar of Lebanon (300 feet high) and instead it became a four-foot shrub. Here, instead of a glorious banquet, the house ends up full of undesirables and street people.

There is a progression: first come the disabled and the oppressed; afterward come the prostitutes, pickpockets, tax collectors, and all the disreputable riffraff of the town. These are the people who finally show up for the dinner.

At this point the average hearer is quite uncomfortable. The prophetic text of Isaiah about the messianic banquet has been completely undermined. Let us recall the description of Isaiah:

> On this mountain the Lord of hosts will make for all peoples a feast of rich food, a feast of well-aged wines, of rich food filled with marrow, of well-aged wines strained clear. And he will destroy on this mountain the shroud that is cast over all peoples, the sheet that is spread over all nations; he will swallow up death forever. Then the Lord God will wipe away tears from all faces, and the disgrace of his people he will take away from all the earth, for the Lord has spoken. It will be said on that day, Lo, this is our God; we have waited for him, that he might save us. This is the Lord for whom we have waited; let us be glad and rejoice in his salvation. (Is. 25:6–9)

The feast and the celebration of the meal in this text of Isaiah clearly symbolizes a mighty victory over the Lord's enemies. He will vanquish the ruthless nations and the oppressed people of God will be restored to honor by their all-powerful God. Such is the principal theme of the passage; the problem is that it does not happen in the parable.

In the local villages of the time there was no chance for upward mobility. It was a closed society. Having been rejected by his peers, the householder has to choose between canceling the dinner or inviting others that he would never have thought of asking. In the messianic banquet foreseen by Isaiah, God raises the oppressed people to God's own status and destroys all their enemies. In Jesus' parable, the householder does not raise up the oppressed but joins them in their various forms of human misery. Instead of a vindictive triumph over Israel's enemies, the bottom line is that the kingdom of God as Jesus proclaims it is being celebrated with the destitute and with sinners.

In other words, the kingdom is to be found not in a dinner for the rich and famous, but in table fellowship with the poor, with people of no account, and with those who hang out on street corners. These are the people who in fact finally take part in the dinner. In this remarkable parable Jesus opens a window on the nature of his Father. The celebration of the salvation of God, symbolized by the dinner, is not taking place with the big shots, the well-to-do, and the successful — they declined — but is taking place with the poor, the weak, the ignorant, the oppressed, and those afflicted with physical, emotional, and spiritual pain. That is, in soup kitchens, bread lines, ghettos, and in places where nobody wants to go.

The expectation of the hearers is completely subverted. Just as in the parable of the mustard seed, there is no cedar of Lebanon, so here there is no great dinner. It is our desperate need that attracts divine mercy, not our virtues or anything else.

Can we accept a God who becomes so vulnerable as to join the human condition exactly where it is, or more precisely, exactly where we are — in the midst of our impure motivation and behavior? God comes to those who consent to come to God with their lives just as they are. The life and death of Jesus is the actual working out of what it means for God to become a human being.

13

THE PARABLE OF
THE WORKMEN IN THE VINEYARD

"For the kingdom of heaven is like a landowner who went out early in the morning to hire laborers for his vineyard. After agreeing with the laborers for the usual daily wage, he sent them into his vineyard. When he went out about nine o'clock, he saw others standing idle in the marketplace; and to them he said, 'You also go into the vineyard, and I will pay you whatever is right.' So they went. When he went out again about noon and about three o'clock, he did the same. And about five o'clock he went and found others standing around; and he said to them, 'Why are you standing here idle all day?' They said to him, 'Because no one has hired us.' He said to them, 'You also go into the vineyard.' When evening came, the owner of the vineyard said to his manager, 'Call the laborers and give them their pay, beginning with the last then going to the first.' When those hired about five o'clock came, each of them received the usual daily wage. Now when the first came, they thought they would receive more; but each of them also received the usual daily wage. And when they received it, they grumbled against the landowner, saying, 'These last worked only one hour, and you have made them equal to us who have born the burden of the day and the

*scorching heat.' But he replied to one of them, 'Friend, I am
doing you no wrong; did you not agree with me for the usual
daily wage? Take what belongs to you and go; I choose to give
to this last as I give to you. Am I not allowed to do what I
choose with what belongs to me? Or are you envious because
I am generous?' "*

(Matthew 20:1–15)

The householder was not generous in regard to the wages
he offered to the first workers, which was only a denarius,
the subsistence wage for peasants. They worked a twelve-
hour day in the scorching heat.

At intervals during the day the householder went to the
marketplace and hired more people. This time he did not ne-
gotiate. He simply said, "I will pay you what is right." There
was no contract, just the hope that he would give them some
reasonable remuneration. At the eleventh hour he went out
again and found a few idlers who had been hanging around
all day. By this time a good number of them were probably well into their cups. So they stumbled into the vineyard,
picked a grape or two, and then it was time to quit.

The householder says to the steward, "Pay the last ones a
denarius." This seems like a sign of great generosity on the
part of the householder. But his generosity runs out when
the ones who worked all day come forward only to get
the same amount. They grumble because they expected to
receive more.

The householder's behavior seems unjust. The hearers
would naturally side with the workers who felt they were
mistreated, even though they received what they contracted
for. This parable raises questions about the standard of justice in the kingdom of God. Should not those who worked
more hours have been given more? Evidently, entry into the
kingdom of God is not a question of merit.

Human standards of judgment are subverted in this parable. Ordinary standards of justice cannot explain how the kingdom works. Paul discusses this problem at length in the third chapter of Romans where he points out that God does not distinguish between persons. Justification and sanctification are gifts and have nothing to do with social status or personal merit. The teaching of this parable is extremely important for those on the spiritual journey. Over centuries a secular standard of values crept into Christian teaching in the form of an elaborate system of earning heavenly rewards. Hence if we were trained in pre-Vatican II Catholicism, we might feel challenged or even dismayed by this parable. We were taught that by going to Mass on Sunday, spending time in prayer and spiritual reading, frequenting the sacraments, giving alms during Lent, abstaining from meat on Fridays, and so forth, we would pile up merits so that the punishment due to our sins would be canceled out. That teaching has been downplayed since the Second Vatican Council, but the temptation remains for people on the spiritual journey, particularly if their experience of prayer is going well. If we enjoy special favors, we might be in great trouble. We might slip into the presumption that our good deeds had earned those gifts. Hence the necessity of trusting in God's mercy and not in our own spiritual experiences or accomplishments.

How do we get into the kingdom if it is not something that we can earn? We enter the kingdom not by meriting but by consenting to the invitation. In the parable, grace is symbolized by the mysterious need of the householder for more workers, and it seems to be urgent, manifested by the fact that he went out every couple of hours to find more workers. Those who accepted his invitation entered, and at the end of the day all received the same recompense. Grace is God's need to respond to our need. The inner nature of God is thus made manifest to us: God has to respond, so to speak, to our needs. In this parable God's response is directed to the people standing there in the marketplace, idle and wasting their time, gambling, drinking, gossiping, snoozing, or whatever.

Jesus in this parable seems to be trying to justify his practice of reaching out to outcasts and sinners. Their behavior does not merit anything, but their need is great. It is their need that he, as God's son, is responding to. Hence his behavior subverts our idea of how to win God's favor. We do not. God's favor and mercy is evoked in direct proportion to our destitution — to our lack of inner and outer resources. Our need is what creates God's need to reach out to us, even if we do not realize how needy we actually are.

The invitation of grace to enter the kingdom goes forth again and again and again. No one is forced to accept. The invitation is extended because of the total largesse and goodness of God. The very definition of mercy is that it responds to need. Infinite mercy of its very nature has to reach out to need. God's greatest gift (response to our need) is, of course, to offer us the divine life itself. This is why Jesus reached out to public sinners. In manifesting the heart of the Father, he had to show the Father's urgent concern for those most in need of his grace and help. Grace and help, of course, are just as gratuitous for the well-behaved.

Respectable folks in general do not like this parable. By respectable I mean those who observe the norms of conventional society, but who are unaware of how much their unconscious programs for happiness are at work in their lives, and how significant a part of their good deeds are secretly motivated by the desire for acclaim, power, or security. The false self easily adjusts to whatever our cultural mindset may be and co-opts good deeds as easily as the not-so-good. On the spiritual journey we need to be alert to our secret motivation. Although self-knowledge does not cure the disease, at least it disposes us to work toward healing, because it shows us the harm we are doing to ourselves and to others.

In trying to face the dark side of our personalities, mixed motivation, and the damage done to us in early childhood, our attitude toward our very real limitations is more important than their healing. Indeed, it is a major part of our healing.

The bottom line of this teaching is that the kingdom is not based on human standards of justice and equity, but on the infinite mercy of God whose principal need is to respond to the desperate state of the human condition.

The fallen human condition is where the kingdom is most active. We are the people for whom Jesus Christ has come in the flesh to express the infinite concern of the Father for our sins and their consequences. The spiritual journey enables us to appreciate more and more the total gratuity of the divine goodness. Acceptance of the invitation is the key to belonging to the kingdom. We are not prize packages. We recognize that boundless compassion is the way God is. It is because God is our Father and Mother that we are invited into the kingdom. That is why our self-generated projects for holiness are questionable and why we need to cultivate a disposition of receptivity and openness to the Holy Spirit. Reason will not get us there. Good deeds will not get us there. The kingdom is sheer gift.

The problem of a faithful and virtuous life, as Scott points out, is that it creates the sense of having earned something from God and thus misses the invitation. Justification does not come through good works but through the divine largesse. Good deeds are essential, but only insofar as they manifest our good will. Spiritual progress is the sheer gift of God. God is not waiting to crown us with a halo for our good deeds. God is waiting to forgive us for our sins and press us to heart as little children in desperate need of boundless love. This parable announces that human standards of judgment have no place in the kingdom. A new standard is present, which is God's infinite need to show mercy.

14

THE PARABLE OF
THE HIDDEN TREASURE

"The kingdom of heaven is like a treasure hidden in a field, which someone found and hid; then in his joy he goes and sells all that he has and buys that field." (Matthew 13:44)

The word parable means "laid beside." So the kingdom of God is known by laying it beside certain symbols or signs. Unlike a simile, the parable actually *contains* the truth revealed by the comparison. Hence the parables are not just comparisons or something like something else. The kingdom really *is* the way that Jesus presents it.

Here the kingdom of God is presented as a treasure. That in itself is not unusual. In the book of Wisdom, wisdom is looked upon as a treasure that has to be sought. But what is unusual — and problematic — is what happens in this parable once the treasure is found.

The man in this brief tale was probably a day laborer. In those days, people did not always have a bank handy. Because of the vicissitudes of the times, they sometimes hid their treasures in a field, hoping to return later in a period of peace to dig them up. Thus it was not unusual for a day laborer working in somebody else's field to come upon a buried treasure. This man hid the treasure again, and then went off and bought the field. The hearers are left with the problem of evaluating the morality of his conduct. If he owned the field, there would be no sense in hiding the treasure. If he had a just claim to the treasure, why would he hide it again? There is clearly an element of scandal in his behavior.

How can the kingdom of God be compared to a treasure that gives rise to such improper conduct? In rabbinical law, if it was not clear who owned the treasure, the owner of the field was presumed to own it. Evidently this man hid it because he was trying to conceal it from its rightful owner.

In the more elaborate version of this parable in the Gospel of Thomas, after the man buried the treasure, he becomes a money lender. So we may think, "Finding a buried treasure for this man must be like winning the state lottery today." Although the lottery is not a buried treasure and one never really expects to win, somebody, in fact, always wins. In any case, this parable is about a similar situation. The treasure is there before the man finds it. This is an important aspect of the kingdom of God. It is in the world and available through the preaching of the gospel. Thus we might find it without intending to — by accident, so to speak.

This man had no test of his virtue but simply found the treasure. His capacity to make good use of his find was thus based on a shaky moral foundation. God has taken a similar risk with each of us. The Father has made the treasure of grace available through the incarnation of his Son, Jesus Christ, but we do not know how to use it. In fact, we are not even remotely prepared for the responsibilities that this treasure involves. Hence we may use the treasure improperly, or the treasure itself may become a scandal for us.

The man in the parable in his joy went and sold all he had and bought the field. Once it is safely concealed in the field, he cannot dig it up again without people wondering how he got it. Though he has the treasure, he is more impoverished than before, because he has now sold all his other possessions. He winds up with an enormous treasure that he cannot do anything with.

The parable alerts us to the fact that the kingdom, although it is given us as sheer gift, is not given to us just for our personal benefit. To share this gift with others is an essential part of receiving it. Not doing so will engage us in some form of scandal, especially if we try to use it only for ourselves.

Since the kingdom comes to us as a great treasure without our having earned it, we do not value it in the same way that we would if we had been forced to seek it. The scandal, then, is that God freely gives us such an abundance of grace that we do not place enough value on it and fail to grasp our responsibilities to make use of it for the community. The treasure, when not used for others, becomes a source of scandal for us. If we use it for purely selfish motives, all the ways in which the false self manifests itself in worldly ways under a religious or spiritual disguise are examples of how the kingdom can become a scandal for us.

This parable is a counterpoint to the parable of the workmen in the vineyard. We saw there that the kingdom comes as sheer gift. We do not earn it, but receive it. This parable reminds us that once we have received the kingdom, we must assume the responsibility to share it with others. From this perspective, the parable is similar to the parable of the talents, in which one of those to whom the householder entrusted his money hid it in the ground instead of taking the risk of putting it out at interest. He was condemned as a worthless servant.

Notice the subtlety of this teaching. This God of ours, like the father of the prodigal son, is always taking us back no matter what we do. God's largesse is boundless. But that very goodness involves a risk. The risk is that we treat the divine mercy as cheap grace, because we have done nothing to seek it or to earn it.

In the mythologies of the various world cultures, the hero is always put to a test before he gets the treasure, the beautiful girl, the Holy Grail, or whatever the reward of the heavy trial. The hero has to slay the dragon to get into the cave or wherever the treasure is sequestered. All of those myths suggest that we do not access the greatest treasures of life without seeking for them ardently and passing through enormous tests. Having been through the appropriate test, we can then handle the treasure.

In Christianity the risk is that the treasure of eternal life is given without our seeking it. It is already there. The kingdom is among us and within us. It is a treasure that involves our participation in the divine life, to which no other conceivable good can compare. And for all practical purposes, most people are not interested. Thus if one receives it at the eleventh hour without having borne the heat of the day, the gift may not be adequately valued. Or if it is highly valued, we may make use of it in worldly ways for personal gain, whether for material profit, as in the case of the man in Thomas's Gospel, or simply by burying it so that no one else can get it.

Finding a treasure exempts us from everyday life. That is why this man experienced such joy, the joy of coming upon a great treasure without having to look for it and without having to work for it. Everyday life for most people requires earning a living. The treasure dispenses us from that. In the parables, the miracle is always muted and usually involves only moderate success after a string of failures. In the parable of the man who sowed seed, we hear about three dismal failures before the seed finally begins to take root and grow. But the final success of the seed consists in an ordinary harvest, not the superabundant and grandiose harvest that would go with the popular idea of the kingdom of God as triumphant.

The gospel reminds us that what takes us out of everyday life is hazardous. The grandiose appeals to our worldly programs for happiness. But the kingdom is not there. It is not in the lottery, even if we win. People love miracles and the extraordinary. The real response to this treasure is to discover the God of everyday, the God of the ordinary, the God who manifests the kingdom in the unclean and what may seem in our judgment to be scandalous.

When the spiritual journey becomes an inner treasure, we want to give more time to prayer, silence, and solitude. We do not want to be disturbed by the cares of the world. There is nothing wrong with this desire in due proportion, but to try to maintain our own peace of mind for selfish reasons, such as avoiding the problems of others, is to fail to understand the chief responsibility of the kingdom.

The parable of the hidden treasure reminds us of what can happen if we treat the free gift of the kingdom as something just for ourselves, or something that dispenses us from the duties of ordinary daily life and the labor of finding God's kingdom in it. In sharing the treasure of the kingdom, one increases one's grasp of it. The kingdom dissolves the monumental illusion that God is somehow absent from our lives or from our prayer. Faith penetrates the psychological experience of prayer and the ups and downs of everyday life, and keeps us directed toward God in the midst of all that happens. This is to respond to the treasure freely given. If we make some mistakes, we are not to let that bother us, not even if we make a fiasco of our whole life. God is not interested in vindicating rights, but in persuading us to be merciful to each other. The Father, whom Jesus reveals, loves us without any conditions and without ever getting tired of receiving us back when we fail.

15

THE PARABLE OF THE UNJUST JUDGE

"In a certain city there was a judge, who neither feared God, nor had respect for people. In that city there was a widow who kept coming to him and saying, 'Grant me justice against my opponent.' For a while he refused; but later he said to himself, 'Though I have no fear of God and no respect for anyone, yet because this widow keeps bothering me, I will grant her justice, so that she may not wear me out by continually coming.' " (Luke 18:2–5)

A parable is a pearl of wisdom set in a particular context by the evangelists for pastoral purposes. We have to remove the jewel from the context in order to get to the heart of the reality proposed by the parable, which shocks us into an experience of who we are and what motivates our conduct. The parables give insight that is not just knowledge, but the knowledge impregnated by love that Paul keeps referring to in his epistles.

Leaving out the context in which Luke places this precious gem, which makes of it an exhortation to pray always and not lose heart, the original meaning of the parable emerges stark and clear.

The outraged widow is not presented as virtuous or having a just cause. The judge is obviously not impartial or objective. How can the kingdom of God be similar to anything in this rather scandalous situation? If the judge was a professional crook, it would not be so bad. But he is supposed be a decent man who does justice to people. The fact is, he is a wretched man!... But the widow keeps knocking.

Let us translate this story into a contemporary scenario. Let us say that there is a judge who is supposed to decide a difficult insurance case. The plaintiff, a widow, who is destitute, sends him two or three letters a day, plus a couple of telegrams, makes innumerable phone calls, endless faxes, and has her friends calling in daily to recommend her cause and demanding justice. When he tries to leave his house or place of work, she accosts him. Regularly she sends him a bouquet of roses with the message, "I'm waiting." Finally the judge cannot stand her constant importuning anymore and without considering the merits of the case, decides to give her all that she wants.

Having concluded the parable, Jesus walks off down the street with his disciples.

With whom can the hearers identify in this parable? Nobody wants to see himself or herself as the unjust judge. Nobody wants to be the destitute widow. Whom can they identify with? That is the crux of the challenge.

The parables are mirrors in which we are invited to look at ourselves. We are the unjust judge. The widow represents the kingdom of God — grace that is constantly banging on our door, morning, noon, and night, pleading, "Do me justice." Or more specifically, "How about spending some time in prayer? How about forgiving your enemy? How about seeking reconciliation with the members of your family? How about helping someone in need?"

Or again, "Accept the dark side of your personality. Take note of the feelings that hinder your relationships, your efforts to forgive and not to judge. Where are they coming from?" These are the things that the divine widow has in mind when she pleads, "Do me justice!" In other words, "Be compassionate as your heavenly Father is compassionate."

The divine widow keeps pounding on the door of our hearts day after day as, like the unjust judge, we try to put her off. If modern forms of communication can be over-whelming, wait until you encounter how many ways of communicating God can come up with. God approaches us all day long, coming to meet us morning, noon, and night through people, events, and our own thoughts, feelings, memories, and reactions. We accept the kingdom finally, not because we are just or deserve it, but because at some point like the unjust judge, we cannot stand the importunities of grace anymore and are forced to give in, saying, "Okay, take my life. I am in your hands."

CHRIST THE KING

16

CHRIST THE KING

Pilate said to Jesus, "Are you the King of the Jews?" Jesus answered, "Do you ask this on your own, or did others tell you about me?" Pilate replied, "I am not a Jew, am I? Your own nation and the chief priests have handed you over to me. What have you done?" Jesus answered, "My kingdom is not from this world. If my kingdom were from this world, my followers would be fighting to keep me from being handed over to the Jews. But as it is, my kingdom is not from here." Pilate asked him, "So you are a king?" Jesus answered, "You say that I am a king. For this I was born, and for this I came into the world, to testify to the truth. Everyone who belongs to the truth listens to my voice." (John 18:34–38)

In our time we think of kings as dictators. In other words, we have a new name for the same old thugs.

Most kingdoms or dictatorships are concerned with sovereignty, power, and domination. These are the connotations of any kingdom or dictatorship that comes to mind, or any kind of community in which the leadership views authority as domination. In many places in the gospel, Jesus challenges that attitude and makes it clear that his kingdom has nothing to do with sovereignty, power, or domination. It is just the opposite.

The kingdom is not like any kingdom that we know of. Jesus said to Pilate, "My kingdom is not of this world." It is indeed a kingdom — that is to say, a community. It has its purposes and structures, but they have a very different spirit and motivation from those of the kingdoms of this world.

The truth to which this kingdom points is that the God of the universe, the ultimate reality, is the Father of infinite compassion and concern for every living thing. This is a revolutionary idea for human beings. Most people live in situations that are more or less oppressive and in varying degrees of interior turmoil, because they do not know how to deal with their frustration. Our false self — the apparatus for self-centered projects for happiness — places us in a continuous double bind. How can we believe in God's infinite compassion and concern for us when we are experiencing some form of oppression, continuous disappointment and frustration, and failure in everyday life? "What is the matter with this God whom we worship?," we ask. "Why doesn't he defend me and provide for me and others better than he does? Isn't this what kings and dictators are for?" Actually, kings and dictators only offer an illusion of security, a vain hope that hides the basic uneasiness of everyday life, which is that we are not secure, not loved as we would like, and not in complete control of anything including our lives and our deaths.

This kingdom to which Jesus bears witness addresses the human condition exactly where it is and says in effect, "It's okay to be weak, broken, even sinful, as long as you accept yourselves and your condition for the love of God." This is the wisdom that Jesus refers to when he proclaims in the beatitudes, "Oh, how happy you would be if you were poor." The people of his time had just as much trouble with that statement as we have today. Poverty does not look like happiness to us, and few have any aspiration to become a part of it. In his day, external poverty was believed to be a sure sign of God's punishment. Jesus totally rejected the popular conception that poverty, oppression, or difficult situations bear any relationship to divine judgment. They are simply the way things are. The acceptance of our particular situation is the beginning of wisdom. It is the starting point on the road to happiness.

On one occasion Jesus experienced ecstatic joy and cried out, "I praise you Father in heaven, because you have hidden these things from the wise and prudent and revealed them to little ones" — ordinary folks, the insignificant, nobodies (Matt. 11:25–30). We may not think insignificance, poverty, and persecution are such great ideas. But Jesus states clearly that those who suffer these things belong to the kingdom that he is introducing into the world. God has identified with us just as we are.

If Jesus' kingdom were "of this world," he would certainly have been rescued by his disciples. If the gospel needed to be vindicated by a show of power, his trial and execution would have been the moment to provide it. The fact that nobody came to Jesus' rescue, even though he could have called upon legions of angels to defend him, is a good indication of the nature of this kingdom. It means that the kingdom is present without our being rescued from our difficulties and the consequences of our sinfulness.

God is present in our lives and deaths just as they are. Whatever happens, the divine presence and action — not as we would like it to function, but as it actually functions — is secretly changing, not the painful circumstances of our lives, but our attitude toward them. In this kingdom we experience our brokenness and our trust in God rather than our virtue and our trust in ourselves.

This does not mean we should not work to resolve our problems and those of others, but rather that we should not try to change other people and the world as if we were divinely appointed to do so. We change the world by accepting it as it is and by helping other people to change by accepting them as they are. The chief work of the transforming attitude of openness to God's will enables us to change. The secret power of the Holy Spirit, totally in the service of infinite love, is working beyond appearances to bring about the final triumph, not of our particular interests, but of the kingdom of God. The kingdom of God, filled with this love, does not depend on support systems that we regard as essential for our happiness. The love of God is the heart of the universe, the meaning of all creation: it is happiness.

The kingdom to which Jesus bears witness by becoming a part of the human condition and by identifying with our suffering and dying, reveals the ultimate truth about the God of the universe, which is that God is completely together with us on every level of our being. God's presence and care are greater than anything we can imagine and much more substantial than anything we can contrive. This reassurance is available whoever we are, wherever we are, whatever is happening, on only one condition: our consent — the consent of faith in the infinite mercy of God. Interior turmoil and the external vicissitudes of life do not interfere with divine union. The gift of wisdom empowers us to find God in our helplessness, weakness, and sinfulness. This is the source of Jesus' ecstatic joy at the thought of how his Father brings to perfect happiness such hopeless and helpless creatures as we are, who are always at one another's throats when we should be in one another's arms.

17

THE REJECTION AT NAZARETH

He came to his hometown and began to teach the people in their synagogue, so that they were astounded and said, "Where did this man get this wisdom and these deeds of power? Is this not the carpenter's son? Is not his mother called Mary? And are not his brothers James and Joseph and Simon and Judas? And are not all his sisters with us? Where then did this man get all this?" And they took offense at him. But Jesus said to them, "Prophets are not without honor except in their own country and in their own house." And he did not do many deeds of power there, because of their unbelief. (Matthew 13:54–58)

This text describes the dismal reception that Jesus received in his hometown. His relatives and acquaintances could not figure him out. Here was someone who grew up in their hometown, who went to their schools and synagogues, and who earned his living as a carpenter. Now all of a sudden, he turns into a wonderworker and starts telling parables that nobody can understand.

There is always some uneasiness when someone we know suddenly becomes a celebrity. We do not know what to do with the situation. We may enjoy basking in the reflected glory of celebrities, but a wisdom teacher is something else because such people are generally confrontational.

Remember the movie *Oh God?* In the film the hero is visited by a divine personage and immediately becomes a celebrity. His friends cannot figure out what has happened to him. The film brings to mind how local friends and relatives must have felt about Jesus. On one occasion his relatives came to rescue him from his preaching ministry because they thought he was going mad.

Ministry, especially a good one, is a losing game. Paul details the long list of his difficulties, including "a thorn in the flesh" that was interfering with his peace of mind. He kept praying to God to free him from the problem. One would think that God would respond favorably to such a great apostle, make things a little easier for him, or even provide him with the red carpet service. Paul was traveling all over the known world of his time spreading the kingdom of God, and what does he get? Shipwreck, imprisonment, stoning, rejection, persecution, and the betrayal of false brethren. Why could not God, infinitely powerful, do something to smooth the way for the divine message?

Difficulties are a stumbling block for everyone, especially when one is working for God. We cannot get enough money, enough help, a decent reception. If we finally get a good crowd, it snows or there is a hurricane, and nobody can come. This God of ours is not predictable. This is what the parables point out. They try to prepare our minds for a different set of expectations from the ones we bring with us from early childhood, and which social custom and even our religious group support.

Paul was thinking, "I'm working for you, Lord, risking my life for you, and this sting of the flesh is getting me down. Can't you do something about it?" There has been much scholarly discussion about what this "sting of the flesh" might have been. It was not an abstract problem; it was in his flesh. Maybe he had arthritis. Maybe he had an emotional problem. Maybe his was an aggressive personality that kept alienating his beloved disciples. Maybe he was impetuous and had a sharp tongue. Maybe he was attracted to beautiful women. Whatever it was, it was serious. He besought the Lord again and again saying, "Let me out of this mess. Help! Help!" And the reply came, "Nothing doing. I prefer the way things are. My power is made perfect in weakness."

This is news. God is more pleased with our weakness than with our success. Why? Perhaps because for most people success is self-defeating. Until we have been squashed, stepped on, rejected, opposed, persecuted, and have endured all kinds of difficulties, success is hard to handle. The experience of our weakness is God's special gift. Paul had great revelations. Great revelations are almost certain to be balanced by great temptations. God is completely just and fair as well as concerned about the dangers of spiritual pride. The bigger the graces, the greater the temptations.

After the divine rejection of his prayer for deliverance, Paul was able to say, "I am going to boast from now on about my weakness so that the power of Christ may be manifest in me." This alerts us to the fact that beyond our ordinary experience of God, with our interpretation of what we think or expect by way of help, is the whole world of divine assistance that takes place in relative secrecy. This world is hidden, but real and much more substantial, affirming, and liberating than events or situations that we are inclined to interpret as God's special blessing or help.

The kingdom of God is active in accidents, disappointments, rejection, and opposition of the kind that Jesus experienced from his own household and that Paul experienced in his weakness. The kingdom of God is in the ordinary ups and downs of life; in the daily routines that bring back the same old weaknesses joined to our inability to overcome them. The presence of the kingdom is manifested in our efforts to keep going, to keep loving, to keep hoping, without any evidence that God is helping us. At the last minute we might find enough money to pay the bills for a month or two. It is life on the edge, life in confrontation with difficulties of every kind. According to Jesus, God identifies with our dilemmas, confusion, struggles, failures. God is present in the sad reflection that after a lifetime in God's service, there is seemingly nothing to show for it. Jesus experienced exactly this kind of situation. He just kept going. If people would not accept him in one town, he went somewhere else. There is always something worthwhile to do in this world. If we get thrown out of this job or that ministry ... so what? *What* we are doing is not as important as our *attitude* toward what we are doing. That is what God is most interested in.

The attitude of faith does not limit God's activities to what we see or feel, but recognizes the divine messages that come coded in the events of daily life. This enables us to say, "I'm not going to fight this problem anymore but make the best of the situation. It may be a necessary remedy that God has sent me to come to know the full extent of God's mercy."

If we are going to connect fully with the mystery of God's love in daily life, our trust in God needs to be unlimited. Once we have let go of our preconceived ideas and prepackaged value systems that expect God to fit into the narrow confines of our human judgment, nothing can separate us from the love of Christ. He keeps breaking out of them and inviting us to come along with him. "Gladly," says Paul, "will I boast of my weakness that the power of God may be fully manifest in me." The power of God becomes greater in the degree that we move beyond our limited ideas of God's action and allow the kingdom to unfold within us.

18

THE RICH YOUNG MAN

As he was setting out on a journey, a man ran up and knelt before him, and asked him, "Good Teacher, what must I do to inherit eternal life?" Jesus said to him, "Why do you call me good? No one is good but God alone. You know the commandments: You shall not murder; You shall not commit adultery; You shall not steal; You shall not bear false witness; You shall not defraud; Honor your father and mother." He said to him, "Teacher, I have kept all these since my youth." Jesus, looking at him, loved him and said, "You lack one thing; go, sell what you own, and give the money to the poor, and you will have treasure in heaven; then come, follow me." When he heard this, he was shocked and went away grieving, for he had many possessions.

Then Jesus looked around and said to his disciples, "How hard it will be for those who have wealth to enter the kingdom of God!" And the disciples were perplexed at these words. But Jesus said to them again, "Children, how hard it is to enter the kingdom of God! It is easier for a camel to go through the eye of a needle than for someone who is rich to enter the kingdom of God." They were greatly astounded and said to one another, "Then who can be saved?" Jesus looked at them and said, "For mortals it is impossible, but not for God; for God all things are possible." (Mark 10:17–27)

Most people, I suspect, feel a certain uneasiness with these words of Jesus. It is not easy to try to translate this challenge into practical daily life. The feelings expressed by the apostles reflect fairly well our own immediate reactions.

Christian tradition has softened the challenge that Jesus gave to the young man. We hear that he looked on this young person with love and wanted him to be his disciple. Christian tradition has emphasized that this saying is not directed to everybody and is not essential for salvation. In other words, to give away everything to the poor and to follow Jesus is a special vocation. Evangelical poverty, it is generally believed, is a special call to the religious life or to a lay commitment to the service of the church.

Personally, I do not think the matter is that simple. Although the literal giving away of everything we own may not be our particular calling, there is a very profound sense in which we have to give everything away in order to enter the kingdom. What is this "everything"? Is it some form of wealth, or is it something more profound? The parable of the rich man and Lazarus (see chapter 4, above) captures that profundity in a remarkable way.

In the parable a very rich man is juxtaposed to a very poor man. The rich man feasted sumptuously every day. The word "sumptuously" means not just well, but luxuriously. Thus he enjoyed a daily banquet with his various hangers-on and friends. Every day for him was Christmas or Thanksgiving. The rich man in the parable was clothed with purple, the symbol of nobility, the upper class, and wealth. At his gate lay a beggar who was desperately hungry. The beggar is described in terms of the utmost destitution. Even the dogs, who in those days were anything but pets, licked his sores.

In the popular mind of the time, poverty and especially

beggary, were looked upon as punishments from God. This was one of the current ideas that Jesus regularly refuted or reversed as in the beatitude, "Blessed are the poor." He also challenged the popular idea that wealth was the reward of virtue. Here he warns his disciples, "It is harder for a rich man to enter the kingdom of God than for a camel to pass through the eye of a needle." That statement wrung from his hearers a cry of despair as they saw their last hope of wealth going down the drain. They murmured to each other, "Who then can be saved?"

Jesus responded, "For God all things are possible," indicating that his example of the camel passing through the eye of a needle is not to be taken literally. It is addressed rather to a spiritual reality. With the help of this parable, we may be able to glimpse it.

Without any discussion of the merits of either person, we learn of the very different situations of the two men in the afterlife. There everything is reversed and an abyss separates them. The barriers that the rich man set up in this life evidently followed him into the next.

The point of the parable is crystalized in the reference to the *gate* of his estate. For the rich man, it was a barrier to keep marauders away from his possessions. The problem for the well-to-do is that the more they possess, the more security systems they need in order to protect their possessions. At the same time, it becomes more difficult for them to pass through the gate. A gate can be a barrier or it can be a passageway to the other. The latter is the secret of the kingdom. It is not the rich man's wealth that is the cause of his future torment, but his mismanagement of it. He failed to grasp that the gift of abundance was not for himself. It had to be shared.

The paradigm of Joseph in Egypt in the book of Genesis (chapter 4) shows us how to make the right use of abundance. Abundance is given for the sake of the community. The kingdom of God is to be in communion with humanity.

Nature of abundance ⇒ sharing wealth & flow
"essence of Community"

It is not a privatized journey. It is manifested in the measure that we pass beyond our personal protective apparatus into solidarity with everyone else, especially those most in need.

Every interpersonal relationship is a gateway to the ultimate mystery and to ultimate human values. What does the gate represent? It signifies identification with the other and with the needs of the other. The gate, the symbol of grace, empowers us to let go of our private world in order to enter into communion with the whole human family. This is what God does. Such is the message of the prophets of the Old Testament regarding the care of the needy, the oppressed, and the poor, who, in the Psalms, are the apple of God's eye.

The rich are not condemned because they are rich. Abraham, in whose bosom Lazarus wound up, is the symbol of the fulfillment of all the promises God made to the people, and he was a very wealthy man. Thus it was not the rich man's riches that were his undoing, but the use he made of them. He made the mistake of thinking that his wealth was for himself. The gate to his estate, instead of serving as a passageway to others, became the barrier that prevented him from entering into solidarity with the beggar and his needs. He could so easily have thrown the poor man a few scraps from his sumptuous table, but failed to do so. Hence he himself created the barrier that prevented him from entering Abraham's bosom.

Elsewhere in the gospel, Jesus affirms that it is more important in a disagreement with someone to leave one's gift at the altar and go first to be reconciled. "Leave the Christian assembly," he says, "until you have reconciled yourself with your adversary." In the kingdom of God, communion is more important than worship. Worship is hypocrisy and a pious sham if we have not first passed through the gate of reconciliation. Thus, mutual forgiveness is presented as the top priority in the gospel. I am not speaking of the feeling of forgiveness, which requires certain psychological steps, but the intention and will to forgive, which may be the best that we can do for now. Jesus reinforces this precept by commanding that we love even our enemies. Any holding back from full reconciliation is to misunderstand the meaning of the gate and the crucial choice of staying inside it or passing through it to others.

The community is the supreme value in the kingdom of God; hence, the importance of how we relate to it. Time is given us to go through the gate and to identify appropriately with everyone and indeed, with everything that is. For all practical purposes, everything that is manifests God. Hence our relationship to ordinary reality reflects our relationship with God. Selfishness, self-centeredness, lock the gate. Even God cannot get in. Communion, which is the gate permanently open to relationship, *is* the kingdom of God. It is available to everyone, rich or poor.

Each of us has an enormous responsibility to share in appropriate ways the abundance of God's goodness to us. If we leave the needy and those we could easily help — physically, emotionally, or spiritually — sitting at our gate, then the gate may follow us into the next life, not as a passageway, but as a barrier separating us from the ultimate communion.

19

THE NEW WINE

Then the disciples of John came to him, saying, "Why do we and the Pharisees fast often but your disciples do not fast?" Jesus said to them, "The wedding guests cannot mourn as long as the bridegroom is with them, can they? The days will come when the bridegroom is taken away from them, and then they will fast. No one sews a piece of unshrunk cloth on an old cloak, for the patch pulls away from the cloak, and a worse tear is made. Neither is new wine put into old wineskins; otherwise, the skins burst, and the wine is spilled, and the skins are destroyed; but new wine is put into fresh wineskins, and so both are preserved." (Matthew 9:14–17)

John the Baptist made quite a stir in Israel and attracted many disciples. Jesus was baptized by him and drew his first disciples from among John's followers. John was austere. He wore a loincloth and ate only locusts and wild honey. He practiced much fasting and expected the same of his disciples.

When there are two spiritual teachers or religious communities in the same neighborhood, the loyalties of one group may conflict with the loyalties of the other. There may be some mutual denigrating and backbiting. Comparisons may be made between *our* observance and their observance, *our* spiritual teacher and their spiritual teacher, *our* tradition and their tradition.

In this incident, John's disciples were sniping at the disciples of Jesus. They said, "How is it that the Pharisees and we fast and you folks do not?" — implying that Jesus' disciples were not measuring up to the high standards of John's. "Who are you" is the implication of the question, "compared with us?" An austere observance draws public attention, admiration, and acclaim.

Jesus graciously adjusts himself to these human foibles. He responds with a question of his own, "How can the wedding guests go mourning while the bridegroom is with them?" By this question he implies that John's disciples are not seeing the whole picture. They are looking for holiness, but in the wrong place. He adds, "When the bridegroom is taken away, then the wedding guests will fast."

He appeals to the fact that his presence among his disciples is a celebration and that it is not appropriate to mourn while attending a wedding. At the very least, they will not be welcome guests. A celebration requires the capacity to receive as well as to give. When God graciously comes into our lives for a few minutes, it is not the time to practice our customary austerities. It is like having a surprise visit from a dear relative who comes to share affection and love, and who finds us too busy with various chores to say anything but, "Come back some other time."

Jesus continues, "Nobody sews a piece of unshrunken cloth on an old cloak. That will only make the rip bigger." And he adds, "People do not pour new wine into old wineskins." An old wineskin dries out, shrivels, and cracks. If we put new wine into it, the chemicals that are still being processed in the new wine will burst the old skin. The old skin does not have the flexibility to expand with the effervescence.

New wine is a marvelous image of the Holy Spirit. As we move to the intuitive level of consciousness through contemplative prayer, the exuberance of the Spirit cannot be contained in the old structures. They are not flexible enough. They may have to be left aside or adapted. The new wine as a symbol of the Spirit has a tendency to stir people up; for that reason, the fathers of the church called it "sober intoxication." Although its exuberance is subdued, it breaks out of categories and cannot be contained in neat boxes.

Jesus points out to John's disciples that they have a good practice but are too attached to fasting as a structure. The wine of the Spirit that Jesus brings will not fit into their narrow ideas. They must expand their views. Otherwise, the new wine of the gospel will give them trouble. It will burst the narrow confines of their mindsets, and both what they have and what they are trying to receive will be lost.

Jesus suggests a solution: "Put the new wine into new wineskins." The new wine of the Gospel is manifested by the fruits of the Spirit, which, according to Gal. 5:22–24, are nine aspects of the mind of Christ. If the new wine is to be preserved, new structures have to be found that are more appropriate than the old ones. If we lean too heavily on the old structures, the new wine of the Spirit will be lost. This happened in the late Middle Ages and especially in the post-Reformation Catholic Church when the emphasis moved from cultivating the fruits of the Spirit to conformity to doctrinal formulas and external observances. That is why we found ourselves at the time of Vatican II in a spiritual desert. The old wine had run out. Renewal in the Spirit, the new wine, is our recovery of the contemplative tradition of Christianity. But this movement of the Spirit has had to be put into new structures; the old ones are likely to burst.

Is it possible to renovate old wineskins? With a lot of greasing they may regain some flexibility, but not as much as new ones. The process may also take a long time.

What will happen with the renewal of contemplative life among lay folks? We will see new forms of contemplative lifestyles that better serve the new wine with its tendency to expand, to excite, and to go to one's head, so to speak. The new wine is the contemplative dimension of the gospel. Its basic act is consent to the presence and action of the Spirit within us. This consent is directed not to our intentionality but to God's intentionality. The Spirit who loves us first is pouring the wine, not we. It is a mistake to think that we have to win God's attention or impress God with our virtues. That is not the new wine. That is an attitude that belongs to the old wine where our virtues are viewed as the necessary means of winning God's favor.

If we consent to God's intentionality, God works in us through the fruits of the Spirit: boundless compassion, joy, peace, and the others enumerated by Paul. No structure can contain such wine. Paul adds, "Those who are moved by the Spirit have no Law." They are beyond any law because they fulfill the purpose of all laws, which is the continuous flow of divine love and compassion. Thus they fulfill every just law spontaneously. ≈ XT's peregrinations

THE COMING OF
THE KINGDOM

20

THE DIVINE GIFTS
The Fourth Sunday of Advent

In the sixth month the angel Gabriel was sent by God to a town in Galilee called Nazareth, to a virgin engaged to a man named Joseph, of the house of David. The virgin's name was Mary. And he came to her and said, "Greetings, favored one! The Lord is with you." But she was much perplexed by his words and pondered what sort of greeting this might be. The angel said to her, "Do not be afraid, Mary, for you have found favor with God. And now, you will conceive in your womb and bear a son, and you will name him Jesus. He will be great, and will be called the Son of the Most High, and the Lord God will give to him the throne of his ancestor David. He will reign over the house of Jacob forever, and of his kingdom there will be no end." Mary said to the angel, "How can this be, since I am a virgin?" The angel said to her, "The Holy Spirit will come upon you, and the power of the Most High will overshadow you; therefore the child to be born will be holy; he will be called Son of God. And now, your relative Elizabeth in her old age has also conceived a son; and this is the sixth month for her who was said to be barren. For nothing will be impossible with God." Then Mary said, "Here am I, the servant of the Lord; let it be with me according to your word." Then the angel departed from her.

(Luke 1:26–38)

At Christmas time children are extremely interested in the possibility of receiving presents. There is a special quality to their expectations that warms the heart. We need to bring a similar childlike expectancy to the liturgy. The Christmas presents that we share are reminders of the incredible gifts of God. The kingdom of God is coming. The liturgy really communicates God's love for us, poured out with extraordinary largesse at each Advent, Christmas, and Epiphany.

In the liturgy the lessons that are read, especially on the great feasts, are not so much instructions in Christian living as demonstrations of grace. The liturgy expresses the effects of our participation in the mystery of Christ by means of events in the Old and New Testaments that typify the gifts we are receiving in the present liturgical celebrations. The celebration of a particular feast thus becomes a parable of the particular aspect of divine light, life, and love that is being transmitted. The heavenly banquet is anticipated in the sacred seasons. In Advent, the kingdom is coming. At Christmas, it is here. At Epiphany, it is manifesting itself to us, in us, and through us to the world.

The common denominator of sacred history is the grace of Christ. In the Old Testament, this grace was offered through types of the good things to come. In the New Testament, these types were fulfilled in the person of Jesus. The same grace is now present in the sacraments and in the Christian community. This fullness of grace is celebrated by emphasizing certain aspects of the mystery of Christ in the course of the liturgical year so that we are not overwhelmed by its extraordinary content and can absorb its unity little by little. Just as we do not survive on only one enormous meal per week, but take a certain amount of nourishment every day, so the various feasts of the liturgical year provide us with the fullest opportunity of assimilating the mystery. Thus faith, hope, and love are increased by the divine communication by degrees, or to use Paul's phrase, "transformed into the same image from one degree of glory to another" (2 Cor. 3:18).

The liturgy is meant to be experiential. Everything that we read about in the Old and New Testaments and all that they symbolize are bestowed not just as information, but as experience. If we stop at mere instruction, we have missed the banquet. The scripture readings reveal the special graces of the day that are being offered for the healing and transformation of every level of our being.

If we come to the divine gifts of the Christmas liturgy with an open heart and an open mind, they are transmitted to us. Recall what they are: divine adoption, anticipation of eternal joy, peace, conformity to Christ, participation in the divine life, understanding of the divine mysteries. The trials of life are not obstacles to receiving it, but test the depth of the transmission. Even the greatest tragedies cannot prevent the triumph of God over suffering. The gifts of the Christmas liturgy point to the life of Christ welling up within us. The divine life within us teaches us not only how to receive but how to give.

In this event we hear how Mary's expectation of her vocation was shattered by the visit of an angel, warning us that the disintegration of our vision of life — disappointments, the heartbreaks, rejection, loneliness, confusion — are part of the preparation for the fullness of our vocation. God never takes anything from us without giving us something better. Sacred history is about how God prepared his people in order to give them the fullness of grace in Christ. Now that this fullness has come, our responsibility is to unpackage the incredible graces that the human family has received and of which we are now the stewards. Our personal history becomes sacred history.

The light, life, and love of God is available in the measure of our receptivity. Each year as we celebrate this opening to the gifts of God, we open more of ourselves to the Lord.

21

THE BAPTISM OF THE LORD
First Sunday after Epiphany

As the people were filled with expectation, and all were questioning in their hearts concerning John, whether he might be the Messiah, John answered all of them by saying, "I baptize you with water; but one who is more powerful than I is coming; I am not worthy to untie the thongs of his sandals. He will baptize you with the Holy Spirit and fire." (Luke 3:15–16)

Now when all the people were baptized, and when Jesus also had been baptized and was praying, the heaven was opened, and the Holy Spirit descended upon him in bodily form like a dove. And a voice came from heaven, "You are my Son, the Beloved; with you I am well pleased." (Luke 3:21–22)

The parables challenge our value systems, conscious and unconscious, thus preparing the soil of our souls for the divine seed, the transmission of grace, which is the kingdom of God. From this perspective, the celebration of the liturgy is the coming of the kingdom.

In the Christmas season, we are presented with one sacred mystery after another. Each one of these feasts has a significance or spiritual meaning. The spiritual meaning is not just an insight but conveys the spiritual power that can change our lives.

There are various levels of spiritual meaning in the celebration of the birth of Jesus, the Epiphany, and the baptism of the Lord, which comprise the Christmas season. As we live longer, we see the mystery at deeper levels. The nature of the mystery is to be both awesome and fascinating at once. We are afraid of it but cannot leave it alone. Faith accesses both the awesomeness and the delightfulness of the mystery.

On the feast of Epiphany, we are presented with the Magi, symbols of seekers of the truth of all time. They arrived at the crib with all their scientific knowledge and were asked to accept as the goal of their long journey an infant lying in the crib making goo-goo eyes at them. The challenge shattered their ideas of wisdom and truth. Their faith, however, triumphed over their expectations. They were able to fall down and worship "God in infant clothing." Such are the facts of the story as presented by the evangelist.

This text describes the baptism of Jesus in the Jordan. How could the Son of God receive a sacrament designed for sinners? What was there to redeem in the redeemer? Yet Jesus submitted to John's baptism of repentance. When John demurred saying, "How can this be? I am not the Christ." Jesus said, "Do it anyway."

Jesus descended into the waters of the Jordan. What was Jesus doing in that muddy river? Since he had no sin, he must have been identifying with ours. This is one of those moments in the gospel when Jesus bears witness to his identification with the human family in its sinfulness, brokenness, tragedy, suffering, and death. If this is the Son of God, then Jesus is telling us that his Father is not just in heaven. He is in total solidarity with human need in its most extreme forms. The heavenly Father is with us just as we are and where we are.

Jesus hangs out with sinners. Thus it is okay to be human; it is okay to be whoever we are. God is in total solidarity with our privation and pain.

The baptism of Jesus is the outward sign of who he is. The significance of his baptism is that he has become one with sinful humanity. On the level of his human nature, he has relinquished his holiness as God's Son and become one of us.

22

THE WEDDING FEAST AT CANA
Second Sunday after Epiphany

On the third day there was a wedding in Cana of Galilee, and the mother of Jesus was there. Jesus and his disciples had also been invited to the wedding. When the wine gave out, the mother of Jesus said to him, "They have no wine." And Jesus said to her, "Woman, what concern is that to you and to me? My hour has not yet come." His mother said to the servants, "Do whatever he tells you." Now standing there were six stone water jars for the Jewish rites of purification, each holding twenty or thirty gallons. Jesus said to them, "Fill the jars with water." And they filled them up to the brim. He said to them, "Now draw some out, and take it to the chief steward." So they took it. When the steward tasted the water that had become wine, and did not know where it came from (though the servants who had drawn the water knew), the steward called the bridegroom and said to him, "Everyone serves the good wine first and then the inferior wine after the guests have become drunk. But you have kept the good wine until now." Jesus did this, the first of his signs, in Cana of Galilee, and revealed his glory; and his disciples believed in him.

After this he went down to Capernaum with his mother,
his brothers, and his disciples; and they remained there a few
days. (John 2:1–12)

The baptism of Jesus signifies his oneness with humanity.
The miracle of changing the water into wine at the marriage
feast of Cana signifies our transformation into Christ. This is
the divine project begun in Advent and brought to completion in the threefold feast of Epiphany. God becomes fully
human so that we may become divinized.

We are invited to look at the final panel of the triptych
of the three events that comprise the feast of the Epiphany:
the coming of the Magi, the baptism of Jesus in the Jordan,
and the marriage feast of Cana. The marriage feast of Cana
is the piece that brings all the rest of the Christmas celebrations to final completion. The divine light that drenched us
on Christmas night, and which we have been gradually ad-
justing to, now reveals the whole panorama of the divine
plan of salvation. The human condition, with its brokenness
and sinfulness, is wiped out in the divine transformation
of human nature, which this panel of the triptych not only
reveals, but communicates to us.

There are three ways in which we grasp the meaning of
the liturgical handling of the gospel texts. The first is the historical meaning — what actually happened. The second is
the significance of what happened. This is usually expressed
in the intention, if we can perceive it, of the inspired author.
Finally, there is the existential meaning of the feast. That is,
what it means in my life.

The feast of the Epiphany focused on the coming of the
Magi, the symbol of seekers of all time, finding the truth they
sought in a most unlikely place — in the face of an infant who
could not even talk. The Magi represent the call of the whole
human race to faith in the infinite mercy of God expressed
in the Word made flesh — flesh in its most fragile form.

The baptism of Jesus in the Jordan is the symbol of purification. He himself did not need the purification but by uniting himself with a human nature and submitting to John's baptism of repentance, Jesus revealed that God is in total solidarity with the human condition just as it is. In other words, Christ is with us in our tragedies, in our sorrows, in our joys, and in our sinfulness to heal all our wounds through the process of the spiritual journey: the sacraments, prayer, and the divine therapy of contemplation.

Here we are looking at a further revelation. It is set in the context of a wedding and described by John the Evangelist as Jesus' first miracle. "There were the six stone water jars for the Jewish rites of purification." Six is the allegorical number of imperfection in the Old Testament. The six water jars symbolize for John fallen human nature, the old creation that emerged out of the waters of chaos.

What is the sacred writer trying to convey in recounting the miraculous change of water contained in these six jars into wine? In another passage John states that John the Baptist baptized with water, but Jesus baptized with the Holy Spirit. Wine with its sparkling, heady, inebriating character symbolizes the Spirit.

Human nature is to be transformed into what wine symbolizes — namely, the Spirit. Notice that the miracle does not annihilate but transforms the water. The wine is not something entirely new; it is a transformation of what was there before. Similarly, our human nature, our personal history, and our self-identity are not annihilated but transformed.

The weddings in Palestine took three days. No wonder the wine ran out! The mother of Jesus was an observant householder and said to Jesus, "They have run out of wine." To which he replied, equivalently, "So what?" John the Evangelist had been a disciple of John the Baptist, who was the great ascetic. It may not have seemed appropriate to the sacred writers that Jesus should perform his first miracle in favor of providing an enormous amount of a substance that John the Baptist would never think of touching.

In any case, the text states that Jesus acquiesced to his mother's concern and changed water into wine. The new wine was brought to the head waiter. He calls over the young man and says, "Everybody serves the best vintage first and after the guests have gotten a little groggy, then they bring out the stuff that's not so hot. But you, dear sir, have saved the best wine until now!"

The miracle implies that the new wine that Jesus provides will never run out. It is also a new creation. The old creation, with its burden of sin is erased, and the new creation, the action of the Spirit, is now available. The new creation is the kingdom of God. And what is the entrance fee? Only the consent of faith. The inherent energy of this wine, strong because it comes from God, will enable us, little by little, to overcome our compulsions, addictions, and sinfulness. Having become one with us in our fallen human nature, Jesus transforms our fallen nature into his divinity.

This is what the liturgy proclaims in this feast. We come to this wedding as guests and we leave as brides. Not a bad exchange, especially if we come as rather disreputable guests. It is the moment in which we understand what it means to be *in* Christ (a favorite term of Paul for incorporation in Christ). The church, that is the people of God, is the extension of Jesus Christ in time. We are the repository of the new wine. We can give to others the old water — our personality, limitations, compulsions, whatever we come to the services with. Or we can give them the sparkling, heady, inebriating wine of sober intoxication. This is the wedding that is now going on but at a level that is not immediately apparent to us until we penetrate by grace and experience the significance of the event.

Wine represents the energy of the Spirit. It is power, but in the service of love. It is too strong to stay in a bottle or in a particular structure. It has to have the freedom to move around and to adjust to circumstances. In this connection, Jesus commanded, "Put new wine into new bottles." The old ones may not be able to contain the chemicals that are being processed in the new wine, whose immense vitality in this case we can only suspect. The one who changed water into wine is even now transforming us into himself through the Eucharist.

EPILOGUE

In the parable of the great dinner, the original people invited did not take their invitation seriously. A similar problem is treated in the parable of the hidden treasure. If we get something for nothing, we tend not to value it too highly. This is the risk that God has taken in inviting us to share the divine life.

In the parable of the great dinner, a symbol of the kingdom of God, we would expect that the householder would get huffy and say, "Since my friends and peers won't come, to heck with the banquet!" He does in fact get very annoyed at the original invitees who did not value his invitation. But rather than cancel the affair, he tells his servants to go out and bring in the lame, the halt, and the blind. Even then the banquet hall is not filled. As a final effort, he sends his servants out to the beat the bushes, so to speak, and bring in anyone they can find, the street people and public sinners. These are the people who actually take part in the banquet. The householder shares the meal with them. Evidently God does not stand on honor but prefers to identify with us and enter into our ordinary lives and deaths, including the scandalous elements in our lives that the leaven in the parable of the leaven symbolizes.

In this way God reveals solidarity with us in the ordinary affairs of daily life, as well as in times and places of monumental corruption whether this be physical disaster, mental illness, or moral degradation. Jesus exemplified the latter by eating and drinking with sinners, which was in his time the sign of belonging to the group with whom one shared table fellowship. The more desperate the need, the more the infinite mercy of God responds by living it with us if we consent.

Christian transmission, then, is not a revelation leading to high states of enlightenment but a participation in the mind of Christ. In this transmission the community — family, local, national, global, the entire universe — is all-important. God is interested in the salvation of every human being and wants us, above every other consideration, to get along together in peace and harmony. If we can believe the teaching implied in Jesus' parables, morality is rooted in this primary concern, and in laws and rules only insofar as they lead to and support the disposition of unconditional love. This understanding is exemplified in the parable of the prodigal son in which both sons treated their father abominably. He forgave them, both without putting either of them to any test of repentance. The transmission of divine life is designed to empower us to think, act, and feel as God does, or at least as God would think, act, and feel if God were a human being. As things are, we have to do that for God.